Surviving & Thriving as a Primary NQT

CRITICAL TEACHING

You might also like the following books from Critical Publishing.

Digital Literacy for Primary Teachers
Moira Savage and Anthony Barnett
978-1-909682-61-0 In print

Inclusive Primary Teaching: A Critical Approach to Equality and Special Educational Needs and Disability
Second Edition
Janet Goepel, Helen Childerhouse and Sheila Sharpe
978-1-910391-38-9 In print

Learning Teaching: Becoming an Inspirational Teacher
Pete Boyd, Barry Hymer and Karen Lockney
978-1-909682-45-0 In print

Reflective Primary Teaching
Tony Ewens
978-1-909682-17-7 In print

Your Primary School-based Experience: A Guide to Outstanding Placements
Second Edition
Catriona Robinson, Branwen Bingle and Colin Howard
978-1-910391-13-6 In print

Our titles are also available in a range of electronic formats. To order please go to our website www.criticalpublishing.com or contact our distributor, NBN International, 10 Thornbury Road, Plymouth PL6 7PP, telephone 01752 202301 or email orders@nbninternational.com.

Surviving & Thriving as a Primary NQT

CATRIONA ROBINSON, BRANWEN BINGLE
& COLIN HOWARD

CRITICAL
TEACHING

First published in 2016 by Critical Publishing Ltd

British Library Cataloguing in Publication Data
A CIP record for this book is available from the British Library

ISBN: 978-1-910391-58-7

This book is also available in the following ebook formats:

MOBI ISBN: 978-1-910391-59-4
EPUB ISBN: 978-1-910391-60-0
Adobe e-reader ISBN: 978-1-910391-61-7

Text design by Greensplash Limited
Cover design by Out of House Ltd
Project Management by Out of House Publishing
Printed and bound in Great Britain by TJ International Ltd, Padstow, Cornwall

Critical Publishing
152 Chester Road
Northwich
CW8 4AL

www.criticalpublishing.com

Contents

Meet the authors

Catriona Robinson is an associate head of the Institute of Education and a principal lecturer at the University of Worcester. She has numerous years of experience working with NQTs in their induction year, both as a teacher educator and as an assistant head teacher at a primary school. In the past she has been involved in the planning and delivery of the NQT events at Worcester.

Branwen Bingle is a senior lecturer and PhD student at the Institute of Education at the University of Worcester. She has mentored NQTs and other colleagues throughout her career as a teacher, literacy co-ordinator, lecturer and researcher, and is experienced in preparing others for the challenges and excitement of classroom life.

Colin Howard is a senior lecturer at the Institute of Education at the University of Worcester and former head teacher. In both roles he has mentored NQTs and has prepared them for the demands placed on teachers who are new to the profession.

Introduction

If you are reading this, congratulations on your appointment as a newly qualified teacher (NQT). We hope that you find your induction period rewarding, supportive, challenging and exciting, all in equal measure. No doubt you are eagerly awaiting the start of your induction period. This book sets out what to expect along the way, concluding with a look forward to what you might expect beyond induction and in your future teaching career. It seeks to reassure you every step of the way and is organised according to the stages of your journey, no matter what time of year you commenced your induction period. You might decide to dip in and out to read about the aspects of induction that are most pertinent to you at a certain time; the book can be read in any order.

The book contemplates the anxieties, anticipation, excitement and some reservations you might have when embarking on your NQT year. A variety of school settings are considered, including academies, middle and independent schools, which have relevance for the majority of educational contexts.

The structure of the book

The opening sections include a useful timeline of activities for your NQT year and 'Unpicking the jargon', which defines regularly used acronyms and terminology. Sources of support are included at the end of the book.

Chapter 1 discusses the period leading up to the commencement of your NQT year. It reviews the first transition point from initial teacher trainee to the beginning teacher role. It looks at what you can do to prepare, including initial visits, how much planning to undertake, what to put up on display, reward systems, and items to purchase. It is made clear that you should strike a balance between being a keen NQT and enjoying what remains of your few weeks of freedom.

In Chapter 2 the importance of the induction mentor is explored. Other types of support networks available to you are signposted, including those available from your Initial Teacher Training provider. Your first Teacher Education Days are considered, with advice on preparation for meetings and what to wear to these events. The chapter also looks at personalising your classroom, its layout, resources, and how to go about establishing relationships with the wider school community. Getting your bearings in new surroundings so you fit in with ease is key.

At the heart of the book is the consolidation chapter (Chapter 3) which draws on aspects highlighted in the early stages of your induction. It reviews planning, assessment, behaviour management and communicating with parents. The nuts and bolts of teaching and learning are evaluated along with pastoral care and wider responsibilities that you will be expected to take on.

Chapter 4 helps you get to grips with the range of paperwork and administrative tasks, including tracking pupil progress, parents' evenings and writing reports. Your working relationships with support staff, colleagues and other agencies are also considered. Additionally, the chapter reflects upon your role in extra-curricular activities, appraisal and inspections.

To conclude your induction period, Chapter 5 examines what outstanding teaching means, professional development opportunities and promotion. It charts the options open to you as you move from your induction period into your new status as a recently qualified teacher (RQT).

Finally, Chapter 6 investigates and prepares you for the more unusual events that you might encounter in your induction period.

Timeline

What to expect during your NQT year

Most training courses include blocks of time in school that enable you to get an overview of the school year. However, it can be difficult to identify exactly when individual schools will expect you to know about particular aspects of practice because each environment is unique. With this in mind, although each chapter is loosely based around when you are likely to experience certain events, you may need to read about the aspects of professional practice contained in Chapter 3 within the first few weeks of beginning your NQT role. Otherwise, an unexpected event such as those discussed in Chapter 6 may happen before you have fully embedded wider school policies. Thus, in addition to the contents list, this timeline can be used to identify where in the book you will find specific information. Each chapter begins with the relevant section of the timeline to enable cross-referencing.

1. Starting to prepare	• Arrange school visit – spend time with your new colleagues and class if possible • Make yourself familiar with school policies and procedures • Familiarise yourself with the induction arrangements in your setting
2. First term	• Get to know your induction mentor and establish expectations • Organise progress review dates and prepare effectively for them • Engage with wider support, eg professional bodies and network events • Become familiar with school policy around parents' evenings and communication with home
3. Second term	• Reflect on your developing practice, particularly planning and assessment • Develop understanding of pastoral care based on mutual respect • Manage behaviour, including tackling issues inside and outside of school • Start being more proactive in taking on wider responsibilities
4. Third term	• Prepare for appraisal and make yourself aware of performance management processes • Reflect on your readiness for Ofsted and/or other inspectorate visits • Think about running extra-curricular clubs, events and opportunities • Continue to develop effective working relationships with other staff
5. Past the post	• Strive to be outstanding through the use of the Ofsted outstanding grade descriptors • Manage your time and workload effectively • Identify opportunities for professional development activities and promotion • Complete your induction period
6. Ongoing considerations	• Look after yourself and safeguard others • Expect the unexpected and manage unplanned events • The Prevent Strategy and other issues of professionalism

Unpicking the jargon

"Those who know, do. Those that understand, teach."
Aristotle

APS	Average Points Scores
ATL	Association of Teachers and Lecturers
B4L	Behaviour for Learning
CAF	Common Assessment Framework
CAMHS	Child and Adolescent Mental Health Services
CPD	Continuing Professional Development
CPRT	Cambridge Primary Review Trust (based on the findings from the Cambridge Primary Review)
DBS	Disclosure and Barring System
DfE	Department for Education
DSO	Designated Safeguarding Officer
EAL	English as an Additional Language
EDAPT	an alternative union for teachers
EHC	Education Health Care
EI	Emotional Intelligence
EPPI	Evidence for Policy and Practice Information
EYFS	Early Years Foundation Stage
HLTA	Higher Level Teaching Assistant
LSA	Learning Support Assistant
NASUWT	National Association of Schoolmasters Union of Women Teachers
NC	National Curriculum
NCETM	National Centre of Excellence in the Teaching of Mathematics
NQT	Newly Qualified Teacher
NUT	National Union of Teachers
Ofsted	Office for Standards in Education
Parentview	Website to consider parents' views regarding their child's school
PPA	planning, preparation and assessment
QFT	Quality First Teaching
QTS	Qualified Teacher Status
RQT	Recently Qualified Teacher
SATs	Statutory Assessment Tests
SDP	School Development Plan
SEND	Special Educational Needs and Disabilities
SENDi	Special Educational Needs, Disability and Inclusion
SIP	School Improvement Plan
STEM	Science, Technology, Engineering and Mathematics
SPTO	Student Pupil Tracker Online
STPCD	School Teachers' Pay and Conditions Document
TA	Teaching Assistant
TeachMeet	an informal meeting between teachers in order to share best practice
TES	Times Education Supplement

1 Starting to prepare: on the starting blocks

'On your marks...'

TIMELINE

Starting to prepare

- Arrange school visit – spend time with your new colleagues and class if possible
- Make yourself familiar with school policies and procedures
- Familiarise yourself with the induction arrangements in your setting

Teachers' Standards

You will have met the Teachers' Standards (DfE, 2011) during your Initial Teacher Training. However, you will be expected to attain each standard at a higher level and further enhance your practice during your induction year. Each chapter begins by outlining the applicable Teachers' Standards. For Chapter 1, these are as follows:

1. *Set high expectations which inspire, motivate and challenge pupils*

    •   *establish a safe and stimulating environment for pupils, rooted in mutual respect*

3. *Demonstrate good subject and curriculum knowledge*

    •   *have a secure knowledge of the relevant subject(s) and curriculum areas*

4. *Plan and teach well structured lessons*

    •   *contribute to the design and provision of an engaging curriculum within the relevant subject area(s)*

5. *Adapt teaching to respond to the strengths and needs of all pupils*

    •   *know when and how to differentiate appropriately, using approaches which enable pupils to be taught effectively*

    •   *have a secure understanding of how a range of factors can inhibit pupils' ability to learn, and how best to overcome these*

7. *Manage behaviour effectively to ensure a good and safe learning environment*

    •   *have high expectations of behaviour, and establish a framework for discipline with a range of strategies, using praise, sanctions and rewards consistently and fairly*

8. *Fulfil wider professional responsibilities*

    •   *develop effective professional relationships with colleagues*

    •   *communicate effectively with parents*

Congratulations

Well done! You have safely arrived at the starting blocks of what will hopefully be a long and very happy career in teaching by securing your first teaching post. You are probably feeling proud of what you have achieved and excited about the prospect of beginning your induction period into the teaching profession. It is quite normal for you to also feel somewhat apprehensive about what lies before you. Although your teacher training course will have prepared you for life as a qualified teacher, having full responsibility for a class of your own brings with it experiences that you may not have encountered before; there will be many firsts in your induction period. For example, you will be expected to organise your pupils' learning environment, label coat pegs and drawers, ensure all the resources your class will need are available from day one and establish mutually agreed class rules with your pupils.

Still looking for an NQT post?

Some of you may still be looking for a permanent position as an NQT. If you find yourself in this position, do not despair but instead utilise this time to your advantage. Look into signing up with a teaching supply agency or teaching recruitment agency. There are many dotted around the country to choose from and further details can be found in the 'Sources of support' section near the end of this book.

While working as a supply teacher on a temporary contract, it is possible to complete your induction period. You can complete the induction period in one school or in three different schools over three terms, for example. This latter option provides you with a wealth of diverse experiences that will show future employers your ability, competence and aptitude to teach in different learning environments. The contents of this book are still pertinent to you if you find yourself in a supply capacity, so please read on.

Using your time effectively

Ready for the start

While you will be keen to get started in your new capacity as an NQT, you should not spend your entire holiday preparing for the start of the term. You will probably want to do some initial planning just for your own peace of mind. Remember though that you need a break before the long haul of any term, especially the autumn one. Plan a few days at the beginning and end of the holiday when you will go into school and then have a good break.

Purpose of school visits

On the day of your interview you probably will not have been able to set up any visits to the school, but the headteacher and governors will be as anxious as you are to organise these. Though the governors will have supported your appointment, it is normal practice to direct future queries about your appointment to the headteacher.

If you do not hear from your school in the few weeks after your appointment it is a good idea to contact the headteacher and ask when would be the best time for you to visit the school prior to starting. The timing will depend on when you have been appointed but most schools will ask you to come in during the latter part of the preceding term. This could be for a single day, such as a sports day or a school performance, or a series of days. Remember that schools are busy places and you might have to talk to the head after the school day in order to organise your visit. This way you can avoid a rushed conversation and have an opportunity to ask simple questions about the timing of your arrival, the purpose of your visit and how much opportunity you will have to talk to your form's current class teacher. Also remember if you are still at university and out on a school placement you must agree any visit to your new school with your current setting and the head of placements at your university so that it does not impact upon you meeting your statutory 120 days needed to gain QTS.

Making the most of your first visit

By now you should have liaised with the headteacher and arranged your first visit. Make sure you leave plenty of time to travel to the school as arriving late will not set a good first impression. It is likely that you will feel nervous as well as excited about the visit but remember to be professional and prepare fully beforehand. This chapter will help you identify the preparation you need to undertake so that you leave your initial visit feeling reassured and confident.

Prior to your arrival you need to make certain that you are clear about the expectations for your first visit. You need to find out if you will be required to teach, work with groups or just shadow the existing teacher. Every school will be different but how you engage with your new school will also to some extent depend on factors such as whether your teaching post is linked to multiple form entry, whether you will work alongside other experienced staff or whether the post you are taking on is the result of a teacher leaving or being moved to a different class. You should also mention that you wish to obtain information about the school and your class during your visit, such as the child protection policy.

You should smile and spend time introducing yourself, in particular to the school support staff such as the caretaker, the school administrator or secretary and the current class teacher. You will no doubt need to contact them in future to arrange access to the building should you wish to visit during the holidays or to clarify any future items with the school office. You should ask them if they are happy providing telephone numbers so that you can contact them should such queries arise both in and out of school hours. Often the headteacher will schedule a time in the day to provide new teachers with important and sometimes confidential information about the school and the new class. This may be the only time you will see your new head so you should think carefully about any questions you need to ask, in particular about contractual information.

Getting to know your class

Your class will be unique and therefore you should spend time finding out as much as you can about the individuals in your charge, the group dynamics, diversity and other useful information that will help you plan successfully. You will need to find out how many pupils are in your class, the gender balance, along with friendships and rivalries.

Consider Jack's experience of his first teaching post below and reflect on what class information you will collect on your first school visit.

CASE STUDY

Jack's experience

I was really excited to have been appointed to my first teaching post but I was really worried about what my new school would be expecting of me on my first visit. I also felt daunted by the newness of it all. When I thought about it, I realised I actually knew very little about my new class, what they would want me to teach when I eventually started or even what time the school day started.

Critical questions

» *What important paperwork do you think Jack should have gathered on his first visit?*

» *What other class information do you believe Jack needed to arm himself with in order to be ready for his first day of teaching?*

You will want to ensure that you know if there are any new pupils due to start, and which pupils have Special Educational Needs and Disabilities (SEND) and/or English as an Additional Language (EAL).

You should spend the rest of the day getting to know your class. Ask for a class list so you can start to learn names and put faces to them. Perhaps ask the teacher to annotate it with any vital information. If the school wishes you to deliver a lesson you should above all make certain that the pupils enjoy it and that it is fun. This is your first chance to make a good impression, which will no doubt be carried home by the children to anxious parents who wish to glean as much information as possible about you as the new teacher. You can use these teaching opportunities to start to gain an impression of your pupils' abilities and characters. You should use one break time to observe them at play so you can again get to understand how they interact with each other. It is also important to spend time in the staffroom getting to know your colleagues and learning about practical issues such as whether you need to bring tea and a mug, alongside any other informal bits of information you can gather about the school and your future class.

Critical questions

» *What other policies will you need to be familiar with in your first weeks of term?*

» *What further information do you need to obtain from the school in relation to your class?*

» *What else do you need to find out while at the school?*

Begin to generate a list of all the information you require in order to start your teaching fully prepared and confident. You could use the checklist at the end of the chapter to prompt you so that you come away from your new school with the most significant pieces of paperwork and information. If you cannot gather all of these items on your initial visit you should make a note to obtain them as soon as possible afterwards.

Getting to know the parents

Many schools will invite you in at a specific time to meet the parents. This may be part of your visit day or on a separate occasion such as a school Parent Teacher and Families Association (PTFA) event, sports day or special assembly. Remember you will be scrutinised so always be aware of what you say, do and wear. Though this is done to help you to get acquainted with parents it also enables the school to allay parents' worries about what their child's new teacher might be like.

This is a chance for you to get off on the right foot with parents so consider how you will approach this. It forms the basis of meeting Teachers' Standard 8 (DfE, 2011), which focuses on how you communicate effectively with parents with regard to pupils' achievements and their well-being. Since this is your first formal appearance there will be a lot to consider.

CASE STUDY

Marcus's experience

I felt everyone was looking at me. I didn't know whether to go up to people or just let them come to me. When talking to parents I was worried I might say the wrong thing, even answering their questions about my teaching background. Some even wanted to know where I would be living and if I had children of my own.

Critical questions

» *How should Marcus have dealt with meeting new parents?*

» *How should he have best answered questions linked to his prior experience or about his personal details?*

You should be proactive and go up to parents and introduce yourself. You should be enthusiastic but a good listener. State how much you are looking forward to starting at the school and teaching the children. Before you talk to parents find out from your new colleagues if there are any children or parents where you might need to put in extra special effort to make them feel they are being listened to or valued. This way you can ensure that during your visit you meet them and spend a moment talking to them about their child.

You should not feel you have to give away too much about your personal life. Be honest but not too specific, such as saying things like you do not know yet where you will be living but that you are looking to buy your first flat on the outskirts of the town. Strike a reassuring tone about your previous teaching experience and tell them how much you have learnt in your career already. Make them realise that you care about children and are passionate about teaching them. You should avoid answering any questions you do not know the answer to such as what trips you are planning next year. Also take care to avoid questions linked to pupils being unhappy with the previous teacher. You should avoid commenting and be non-committal in your responses such as saying how sorry you are to hear this but you have no doubt they will be happy with you.

Planning

During your initial visits to the school you are strongly advised to find out what long- and medium-term planning is available from the existing class teacher. Not only should you be able to leave with hard copies of the plans, it would be sensible to ask questions associated with resources, trips and curriculum subjects that you are not as confident with, etc. You should aim to leave the school with a good grasp of the curriculum you will be expected to deliver when you commence your induction period.

Additionally, you will need to establish if the school uses a particular template for medium- and/or short-term planning. This is likely to be in an electronic format so it would be sensible to take a memory stick with you on your visits. A USB stick will also come in handy for other information such as school policies.

Reward systems

Being at the school for initial visits can provide you with a lot of useful information and knowledge. Of paramount importance is the way in which behaviour (a national priority) is managed. Most schools will have a reward system and you will need to establish what reward system the school uses, for example, zone boards. At the very least you should obtain a copy of the behaviour policy and familiarise yourself with its contents. You will be expected to follow the procedure accurately to ensure consistency across the school and for pupils in your charge. While this policy and its principles have to be followed exactly, you do also have some flexibility in the types of reward systems you can bring to enhance what is already established (Robinson et al, 2015). Therefore, take some time during the period leading into your NQT induction to consider possible reward systems to complement the ones already in use.

Personalising your classroom

Classroom organisation

Though you cannot do a lot before the children arrive, certain tasks can be embarked on with regard to classroom organisation. This will support your development of Teachers' Standard 5 (DfE, 2011), which considers how you might adapt your teaching to respond to the strengths and needs of all pupils.

Firstly, you need to be sensitive to who previously taught in your classroom. It is incredibly easy to get off on the wrong foot by complaining about the state of your classroom and its furniture. Consider the classroom and the furniture and decide how best it might be arranged for your style of teaching and the age range you will teach.

CASE STUDY

Abi's experience

I really want my pupils to enjoy working together though I am aware that I have one pupil who is very sensitive to noise and distractions. I think learning should involve the children investigating as much as possible and I do like to focus on groups when promoting learning. I also do not like queues at the teacher's desk. I like pupils to have plenty of room to move around and be able to easily and independently access the resources they need.

Critical questions

»   *What classroom organisation should Abi consider for her room, and why?*

»   *How might she best allow pupils to work together and have ease of access to resources?*

You could consider setting your classroom out as shown in Figure 1.1.

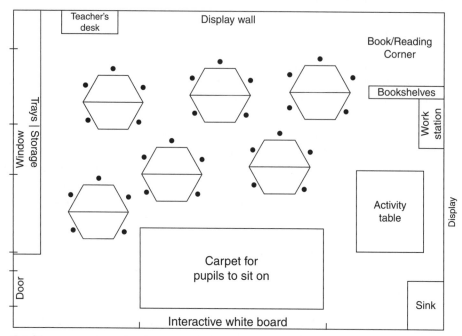

Figure 1.1 *Classroom organisation to support group learning*

This layout allows your pupils to share learning experiences and enables you to work with targeted groups for focused learning. You could make certain each desk has a work tray so that pencils, rulers, rubbers and other resources are easily available. These should be clearly labelled with images as well as words to help pupils with special educational needs. You should also consider either removing your desk or placing it in the corner of the room where it is less obvious. You could think about having an activity/art table set up ready for children to visit independently if they wish to be creative. If any children have individual special needs you could consider setting up a work station for them or a place which can be used and prepared by the teaching assistant (TA) to support their learning. For further information on special educational needs, disability and inclusion (SENDi), see DfE (2014a). If the children have lunch boxes you may wish to set up a storage place for these alongside a dedicated reading corner which children can independently access.

In addition, it is a good idea to display a visual timetable for pupils to look things up on, as well as labelling their drawers and coat pegs ready for the first day. Once the children have arrived, these could be replaced by their own customised labels.

Classroom displays

You will also need to consider preparing your display boards for the term. When completed, these can provide an excellent means of meeting Teachers' Standard 1 (DfE, 2011) which focuses on setting high expectations and providing a stimulating environment for pupils.

CASE STUDY

Poonamben's experience

I was really daunted by the blankness and the state of the wall boards which had small torn remains of yellow backing paper on them. I had been so used as a trainee to not worrying about this aspect of teaching, of seeing someone else's completed display or being told while on my teaching practice what theme to put up on the wall board. I felt panic since this was all mine now and I suddenly realised that I did not know what they wished me to do in order to make my room look lovely again.

Critical questions

»   *How should Poonamben have started to tackle this task?*

»   *What are the important aspects of display that Poonamben should have considered?*

Before you start thinking about your display you should find out if the school has a policy concerning the displays – defining how they should be mounted, for example. Some schools will even state that displays must be kept within the boards and that you should not put up mobiles since it causes issues with the security alarms. It may even be that the school has certain communal areas for which each class is responsible. If so you must make certain you find out when these displays are due to be completed and what the themes will be. You should then check which backing paper and borders may be used from the stock cupboard in case certain stock has been ordered for a particular display or teacher. Then you must decide where you can put up the most effective displays.

If you start your NQT period mid-year this dilemma should not arise as you will inherit current displays. If you start at the beginning of the autumn term then the wall boards will have been stripped at the end of the summer term ready for your arrival and the new class to move in. You need to consider what topics you plan to cover in your first term, which will make for the best display and when they would be best placed for maximum effect given the stock available. You should also decide what static displays you might need such as commercial time-table squares and phonic lists, and displays for working walls. All of these may need backing. Also you should consider whether you wish to have a display table linked to your wall displays and if so how will you cover it. You will need to consider where to put up displays. If you are in a particularly sunny room you need to think whether certain boards will fade quicker due to the bleaching action of the sun. If this is the case you should use commercial posters since they are more likely to survive this bleaching action. Commercial posters can quickly cover a board so as to be inviting for when the pupils start; however, remember to leave some wall space for children's work. Displaying children's work alongside the posters in the first few weeks of your induction will signal that you value what they have produced.

Resources

On the initial school visit or a subsequent visit it is important that you find out which resources will be available to you once you start. Look around the class and in stock cupboards to see what is typically available. You will need to ask what stock your class will be provided with, such as exercise books and pencils, and if necessary ask if particular items could be ordered before term starts. Although most items come quickly nowadays the busy start of a term is not a good time to ask for items, especially if you need them for the first week.

Remember the teacher may take some items with them so ask if there is anything in particular that will be gone. Also check the class numbers to see if you need to find additional seating or desks for the incoming class and if so how to go about getting them. It may be that they come from another class and therefore you will have to wait for them to become available. It is important that you do not spend lots of your own money buying resources for the class. Schools will often reimburse teachers for small purchases but it is important that you ask first since they will need authorising. It is often better to wait and see if there is anything specific you need, such as a science text, and then think about purchasing only if it cannot be borrowed.

What to expect

Teaching expectations

Usually you will be expected to teach for 80 per cent of the week, with 10 per cent non-contact time as an NQT and 10 per cent planning, preparation and assessment (PPA) time. Within your NQT induction period it is unlikely that you will be expected to take on a subject co-ordinator's role. However, sometimes this does happen, particularly if you are in an academy school where employment contracts and obligations differ from those in mainstream schools. Employment contracts are explored in greater depth later in this chapter.

Targets from your final school experience

Although it is tempting to see your training course as behind you now you have QTS, you should use your final school experience report to set yourself developmental targets for your first term. You and your university (or training course provider) tutor will have identified strengths in your practice and areas you need to develop, and it is important that you address these areas at the earliest opportunity. This used to be done as a series of transition points which formed a Career Entry and Development Profile, and some schools may still use this wording to frame the process; others may have developed an induction programme specific to their school.

If the induction process has not already been explained to you as part of the recruitment process, ask who will be responsible for monitoring and supporting your NQT year. It is currently a statutory requirement for maintained schools to put in place '*a suitable monitoring and support programme ... for the NQT, personalised to meet their professional development needs (including the development needs of part-time NQTs)*' (DfE, 2014b, p 17). Although there is no statutory requirement for NQTs in independent or academy settings to complete an induction period, it is possible to complete your NQT induction in these settings.

The main thing to remember is that you will still be meeting the same standards that informed your practice during your training. This means you are already familiar with the strategies you can use to develop your professional practice, but some may be more difficult to implement (such as observing other members of staff now that you have responsibility for a whole class). Team-teaching with a more experienced colleague or a subject co-ordinator is one way you can work around such timetabling commitments; other strategies include:

- asking colleagues how they address particular issues such as behaviour management or scaffolding learning;

- joining professional organisations and subject bodies (see 'Sources of support') and using their research, resources and online forums to seek advice – remembering to remain professional and ethical at all times;

- identifying professional development opportunities such as training courses.

Training courses

Training courses are offered by a wide range of providers to address most educational issues, with new courses being developed all the time. It can be difficult to decide which ones are worth the money for you and your employer. If your school uses a particular teaching scheme it is quite likely that staff training will be included in the fee, and your headteacher should arrange for you to receive the appropriate training as soon as it is available. It is always worth asking if the staff have received training for particular schemes in the past and if it is possible to be sent on a course to help you 'catch up'.

Other opportunities may arise through subject bodies and professional organisations. It is worth being aware, though, that your individual needs are not as great as the staff as a whole. A course that may look very interesting for you personally may not be funded, and you will not be released, because it is not deemed necessary or another member of staff has already been trained in that area. School budgets are finite, so it is also important to investigate what others have said about the opportunities you find: it is worth seeking recommendations from trusted sources, particularly word-of-mouth between colleagues.

The important thing to remember is it is now up to you to keep up to date with the opportunities available as you are responsible for managing your own career. If you maintain the habit of identifying strengths and areas to develop as mentioned in the previous section it will be easier to spot courses that will either help you progress in your career by developing your strengths, or it will aid you in addressing areas in which you want to perform better.

Your NQT school mentor

Once you are appointed your headteacher will assign a member of teaching staff as your designated induction mentor. Usually the member of teaching staff is a member of the senior management team, feasibly the headteacher, deputy or a key stage co-ordinator. Often these individuals have experience of mentoring initial teacher trainees and/or have been responsible for previous NQTs in their school. On occasions, however, aspiring individuals who are new to the role may be selected in a bid to widen their experience and contribute to their continuing professional development (CPD). Whoever is appointed, the relationship you construct with your mentor is paramount and fundamental to the success of your induction or probationary year. This is explored in greater detail in Chapter 2.

Duration

You need to ensure that you agree a start and end date for your induction period. This will depend on the route you took into teaching. For example, if you have completed a PGCE or undergraduate course your induction period will usually last for one academic year if full-time, but longer if part-time. If, however, you have come into teaching through an alternative route, like Assessment Only, then you can complete induction in as little as a term.

Union membership

You are strongly advised to subscribe to one of the teaching unions prior to commencing your NQT induction. You may already be a member of a union in your capacity as a trainee teacher. However, now is an opportune moment to review your subscription as many unions offer enticing rates and offers for NQTs. See 'Sources of support' for further information.

Choosing a suitable union is an entirely personal decision. In the first instance, do your homework. Take time to look at each union's website and consider whether their ethos fits with your values and beliefs. Furthermore, you should be mindful of the subscription rates each union charges and investigate whether they have any additional benefits for NQTs. You are strongly advised to talk to other teaching professionals about their choice of union and then make your decision based on all the information you have gleaned.

You may be asking yourself why there is a need to subscribe to a teaching union, particularly if your political persuasion does not sit comfortably with the notion of unions. Teaching unions are one of your first points of contact should you encounter any difficulties in your induction period and beyond. They will represent you at judicial hearings or at internal appeal committees should the need arise. Furthermore, as an NQT you are entitled to support and guidance from your induction mentor and other school colleagues. On some occasions, support is not always too forthcoming due to other demands placed on schools and their personnel. In these instances, things can start to go wrong, eg a series of poor lesson observations that spiral into you being told that you 'require improvement'. A union would be able to offer advice in these circumstances. The series of support mechanisms available to you are explored in depth in Chapter 2.

Contractual obligations

When you have been appointed to a school, even if a contract has not been signed, once you have accepted your job verbally you and your employer have entered into a legally binding contract. Theoretically, if you change your mind you could be held to this agreement. However, usually in practice this is unlikely to happen since no one would wish to keep someone who is reluctant to be in a school. Your proposed employer could, however, charge you for a re-advertisement of the post and the associated costs of carrying out another interview. Also you would run the risk of having your reputation damaged by such an incident.

After the verbal agreement stage of your appointment, a written contract known as 'conditions for employment' will be issued from the appointing body. This is contractually binding for both parties; once this is signed it cannot be changed without the agreement of both parties. It is also a good idea to ask for your job description, though this is not a legal requirement, which will indicate the duties and responsibilities linked to your post.

Remember it may take some time for you to receive a contract for many reasons. However, under the Employment Rights Act 1996 you have the right to have a written statement of the particulars of your employment and you must receive such a document no later than two months after your employment begins. You should not worry if it does not appear straight after you have accepted your job. If you are concerned you could always contact your school to see if they have submitted the required paperwork and that things are in hand. Alternatively, the human resources team at the local authority may be a good starting point to ease your worries.

Most conditions of employment set out your name, job title and place of work, the employment commencement date, your pay scale and rate of pay, the type of contract (whether fixed term or permanent) and your terms and conditions including hours of work and holiday entitlement (including public holidays).

If you are employed within the maintained sector your terms of employment will be covered by a collective agreement (locally known as the Burgundy Book) along with the school teachers' pay and conditions document (STPCD). This will mean that your pay and conditions will stay constant across the maintained sector. However, if you are employed by an academy, free school or independent setting your conditions of employment will be subject to the collective agreements, policies and procedures established by the employer, ie your school. Though they can often be similar to the maintained sector you must not assume they will be exactly the same, so check. Since pay in academies is not required to follow the national pay scales for teachers it is important that you check what your starting salary will be and how you can ensure progression of pay during your employment. You should also check with your academy what benefits you are entitled to and how long you will have to work to gain these benefits. Finally, since academies have the power to alter the length of a school day and school term dates, you should also make yourself aware of what you have signed up for, including whether your job includes any additional responsibilities and duties.

CHECKLIST

Class information

✓   Class register.

✓   New pupils joining the class.

✓   Details of any medical issues or health care plans for individual children.

✓   Details of individual education plans and/or any pupils with SENDi.

✓   School tracking information regarding pupils' attainment such as reading levels.

✓   Location of your classroom, the hall, swimming lessons etc.

✓ ICT timetables, use of the hall for PE, music etc.

✓ Medium-term planning for English, mathematics, science and foundation subjects.

✓ Exemplars of weekly planning, especially for mathematics and English.

✓ Knowledge of key schemes used to support mathematics and English.

✓ School visits that pupils went on.

✓ Friendship groups.

School documentation

✓ Child protection policy.

✓ Behaviour policy and reward systems.

✓ Marking policy.

✓ Health and safety policy.

✓ Prospectus, if not online.

✓ Staff handbook.

✓ Staff list and contacts.

✓ Subject co-ordinator names.

Other

✓ Review teaching union subscriptions and select one to join.

✓ Join a teaching supply/recruitment agency if still looking for an NQT post.

Further reading

Department for Education (DfE) (no date) *Get Into Teaching*. [online] Available at: www.education.gov.uk/get-into-teaching/about-teaching/induction-year (accessed 8 December 2015).

Teaching unions

Please refer to the respective teaching union websites below for further information on how to join and the support they offer:

Association of Teachers and Lecturers (ATL): www.atl.org.uk/

National Association of Schoolmasters (NASUWT): www.nasuwt.org.uk

National Union of Teachers (NUT): www.teachers.org.uk/node

VOICE: www.voicetheunion.org.uk/

2 First term: ready, steady, go!

Hitting the ground running

TIMELINE

First term

- Get to know your induction mentor and establish expectations
- Organise progress review dates and prepare effectively for them
- Engage with wider support, eg professional bodies and network events
- Become familiar with school policy around parents' evenings and communication with home

Teachers' Standards

The following Teachers' Standards (DfE, 2011) are applicable to this chapter.

1. *Set high expectations which inspire, motivate and challenge pupils*

    • *set goals that stretch and challenge pupils of all backgrounds, abilities and dispositions*

2. *Promote good progress and outcomes by pupils*

    • *be accountable for pupils' attainment, progress and outcomes*

5. *Adapt teaching to respond to the strengths and needs of all pupils*

    • *have a secure understanding of how a range of factors can inhibit pupils' ability to learn, and how best to overcome these*

6. *Make accurate and productive use of assessment*

    • *know and understand how to assess the relevant subject and curriculum areas, including statutory assessment requirements*

    • *make use of formative and summative assessment to secure pupils' progress*

    • *use relevant data to monitor progress, set targets, and plan subsequent lessons*

8. *Fulfil wider professional responsibilities*

    • *develop effective professional relationships with colleagues*

    • *communicate effectively with parents*

Getting to know your induction mentor and establishing expectations

The importance of your induction mentor

Your induction mentor will give advice and support on how to attain the Teachers' Standards (DfE, 2011) at the expected level for someone entering the profession having already achieved QTS. He or she will be a key constituent in your ability to succeed (or otherwise), so don't underestimate their importance in your CPD. It will be important to strike up a purposeful relationship with your mentor, establish your respective responsibilities, know where to turn for support and engage with a mentoring and coaching model so as to enhance your ability to be an autonomous and reflective practitioner.

What makes a good mentor?

Critical questions

» *What would you envisage as key roles, skills and attributes desirable in your induction mentor?*

» What makes for an effective relationship with your mentor?

» How do you think your perception of effective induction mentoring might differ from your mentor's?

You may have listed some of the following attributes.

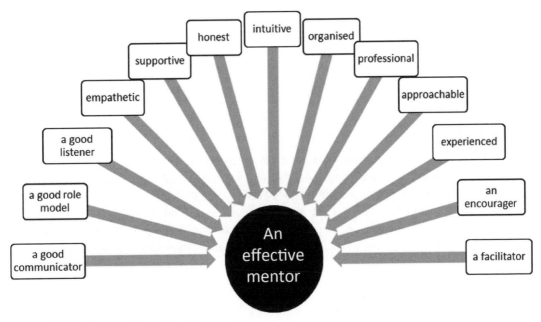

Figure 2.1 *Attributes of an effective mentor*

Of course you may have listed other qualities and characteristics, which are equally valuable and important. However, you should be aware that there might be a discrepancy between your perception of the mentor relationship and that of your mentor. Small-scale research has highlighted this incongruity (Robinson, 2013). For example, you may not believe that experience is necessary to be a good mentor but mentors may regard this as an essential component in performing their duties to the highest standards. What is important, however, is your ability to engage with your mentor, seek out advice when needed (including advice from other staff) and understand the demands made on their time. This will help you strike up an effective working relationship. You may also want to consult the school's induction policy, so that you are aware of the support on offer and get the maximum benefit from your induction period.

The role of your mentor

Your mentor has a variety of responsibilities and roles to undertake within your school setting. Their duty is to assist you in the effective transition from initial teacher through to NQT status and onwards through performance management (see Chapter 4 for further information). DfE (2013a) guidance explicitly outlines the roles and responsibilities of those involved in your induction and you are advised to make yourself familiar with this statutory guidance.

You can expect in the first instance that your NQT induction mentor will be your first point of contact for the year. You should view them as your guru and adviser. Induction mentors are expected to observe you teaching and will monitor and review your progress through regular meetings. Three formal assessment meetings will be convened throughout your induction period, usually once a term, and the discussion will draw on contributions from other members of the school team. If you are conducting your induction period on a part-time basis, this will be pro rata. Your mentor will write your formal assessment record (DfE, 2013a) and ensure that you are aware of the professional judgements made of your performance, inviting your comments in response to these verdicts.

CASE STUDY

Habiba's experience

I was really pleased with the teacher that had been assigned to me as my induction mentor. We got on really well. She was really sociable (we went out on a couple of nights together) and she always asked after my health and well-being on a regular basis. After the first term, however, I started to get concerned. My induction mentor had not observed me teaching but more worryingly I had not had one progress review meeting. As I went into the second term, I didn't know how I was doing, what I needed to do to improve or who I should turn to.

Critical questions

»   *In your opinion what is the role of the induction mentor?*

»   *How does Habiba's tutor fail to exemplify the role of the induction mentor?*

»   *Is there any way Habiba could have avoided this?*

»   *Who should she turn to next?*

»   *How could Habiba have been more proactive in order to alleviate this situation or stop it from arising in the first instance?*

Your relationship with your induction mentor

Clearly striking up a professional yet social association with your induction mentor (and other colleagues) should not be condemned. After all as an NQT you need to have a work/life balance and attending sociable occasions with colleagues outside work time is invaluable in cementing professional relationships and friendships. That said, there is a clear divide between the professional and personal. The induction mentor still has to meet their professional obligations. In the case study above Habiba should have been proactive and initiated regular progress review meetings and lesson observations. Failing this, the next step would be to have a professional heart to heart with the induction mentor to explain how the situation was impacting her professional development. If the situation did not improve, Habiba would need to talk to the headteacher (in the first instance), governors or her Initial Teacher

Training provider. All these stakeholders are catalogued within the statutory guidance and available to help. Finally, if problems with the induction mentor or other aspects of NQT support cannot be resolved, then the last port of call is the appropriate body. The appropriate body is the organisation that is ultimately responsible for your induction period. They will be the body that agrees the recommendation put forward at the end of your induction period.

On some occasions, the headteacher may be your mentor. With the best will in the world, they want to support you and ensure that you become an excellent teacher. However, they too have pressures and commitments arising from managing and leading the whole school. This in turn impacts on the quality of support and time they can apportion to the induction mentor role. Therefore, knowing who to contact from the outset should your induction mentor not be available is of paramount importance.

Maintaining contact with your training provider

Since 2012, and subsequently revised in 2014, the latest Ofsted inspection framework for Initial Teacher Training entrusts providers with NQT responsibilities. They are charged with ensuring that you continue to make progress as an NQT and reflect the standard of teaching exhibited on completion of your training. Therefore, it is highly advisable that you keep your training provider updated of your progress regardless of your situation. It is likely that they will not only welcome your contact but will actively support you in dealing with any tensions during your NQT induction period and offer further training opportunities through tailored sessions. You are advised therefore to confirm your employment details with your provider and actively investigate the training programme they offer for NQTs. There is an expectation that your Initial Teacher Training provider will be able to offer assistance should you require it. For example, if you were struggling to get to grips with aspects of your teaching in your final placement before qualifying, then you should retain contact with your provider who will be only too willing to help and may even offer to visit you in your new job to offer support.

While the induction mentor may not be responsible for providing training opportunities, they should seek to facilitate opportunities for you to meet your induction targets. Clear identification of transitional targets should inform your employer of the sort of training opportunities you require and these should be reflected in your induction action plan. Your induction action plan will be drafted in consultation with your induction mentor from the outset. You should review and update this on a regular basis and share progress updates with your induction mentor when you meet.

More about coaching and mentoring

You are strongly advised to consult Whitmore's (2002) coaching and mentoring model to help you develop your understanding of a purposeful mentoring session. It will also support you in your CPD beyond your induction year in facilitating a reflective solutions-led approach to your teaching. You may want to share this model with your induction mentor in order to establish a common framework for coaching throughout your induction programme. Whitmore's 'GROW' model of mentoring and coaching covers four key areas.

1.　**G = Goal**

What do you hope to achieve? Take time to think, clarify your aims and objectives and how you might achieve them.

2.　**R = Reality**

What is the present situation? What and how great is your concern about it? What resources do you already have? What skills, time, enthusiasm, money, support do you have? What other resources will you need? Where will you get them from? What is really the issue here, the nub of the issue?

3.　**O = Options**

What are all the different ways in which you could approach this issue? What else could you do? Would you like suggestions from your induction mentor? Which solutions are most appealing, or feel best to you? Make a list of all the alternatives, large or small, and the complete and partial solutions.

4.　**W = Will**

Which option or options will you choose? To what extent do these meet all your objectives? What are your criteria and measurements for success? What support do you need and from whom? What could your induction mentor do to support you?

(Adapted from Whitmore, 2002)

The roles and responsibilities of an NQT

Keeping a development portfolio

It is a good idea to arrange to meet with your induction mentor as soon as possible. This enables you to agree priorities for your induction period that will be reviewed on a regular basis. You are entitled to a reduced teaching timetable as an NQT and you should agree with your induction mentor how you will use this non-contact time. Obviously you will be expected to provide evidence of how you are meeting the Teachers' Standards (DfE, 2011) consistently and over a sustained period. You are therefore encouraged to keep a development portfolio, much the same as the professional development profile you will have kept for your Initial Teacher Training. You are advised to regularly update this document and this may be one of the ways in which you use your non-contact time.

Creating an induction action plan

Whatever your targets for induction were, you should have a clear plan of action following your initial meeting with your induction mentor. Your action plan should enable you to meet the agreed targets. You can use the action plan to guide review meetings with your induction mentor when monitoring and reviewing your progress.

CHECKLIST

Golden rules for NQTs and how to work with your induction mentor

✓   Keep a diary.

✓   Be proactive.

✓   Plan how you will use your non-contact time effectively.

✓   Ensure that you gather evidence for the Teachers' Standards regularly and update your professional development file.

✓   Make sure you know who else to contact should your induction not be satisfactory, eg the appropriate body.

✓   Familiarise yourself with the school's induction policy.

✓   Familiarise yourself with the school's performance management process.

✓   Ensure you understand what roles and responsibilities are placed on NQTs.

✓   Identify a range of NQT support networks.

✓   Maintain an induction action plan that you can self-review and share with your induction mentor.

✓   Confide in your induction mentor or someone else that can help at the school if you are having difficulties in your NQT period.

✓   Agree your NQT programme of training events and conferences with your induction mentor.

✓   Ascertain the number of teaching observations you will receive in the course of a term/year.

✓   Confirm the frequency and number of meetings you will have with your induction mentor.

✓   Ascertain the frequency and timings of your formal NQT progress reports.

✓   Discuss a coaching and mentoring model with your induction mentor.

If things go wrong

More often than not, your progress will be smooth and pass without incident. However, sometimes things do not go quite according to plan, either because of professional or personal difficulties. Alternatively, you may encounter difficulties not of your making such as the ones described by Habiba earlier. Consider Cole's experience below.

CASE STUDY

Cole's experience

Wow, I felt elated! I had secured a job as an NQT in the school where I really wanted to work. Things started off really well and I was making great progress. Everyone was really happy with how things were going, including me. I could see that pupils were learning and I had already managed to secure hard evidence to demonstrate pupil progress. But then, everything went downhill rapidly. Firstly, my partner had just returned to work following the birth of our first child. This started to take its toll on the pair of us. She went back to work shifts and it meant that I was often left to go and collect our little boy from childcare. I started to really struggle to keep on top of things, planning became sketchy at best and on some occasions I went into lessons with nothing written down. I was having to leave school early and was arriving in the mornings much later than I wanted. I kept thinking that things would start to improve; it would get easier.

Colleagues started to make comments about my time-keeping. I ignored them, kept going and tried to paper over the holes. To counter their comments I tried to stay as long as possible at the end of the school day, only to find that I was arriving late to pick up Joe and he was becoming distressed. The child carer was also getting fed up with me arriving late from school to collect him. Guilt started to set in too at that point. Nothing I was doing was right. After some weeks, my induction mentor spoke to me about this matter and I made some excuse, apologised and I said I would try harder. Well, I didn't want my induction mentor knowing about my personal business, now did I?

At this point the induction mentor also told me that they would observe my lesson the following week as part of regular progress monitoring. I put on a brave face, but I was worried. When the time came for the lesson observation, I had not been able to give the planning the attention it needed as it had been my week to collect Joe from childcare. I knew the induction mentor had been happy with my work up until that point, so concluded that I could probably 'wing it' without the detailed plan I needed. Then it got ten times worse. My lesson was a disaster! I had not thought through the different resources I would need because I had not planned thoroughly enough. Pupils were disruptive because resources were not available and they certainly weren't learning anything. Oh, it was awful! I ended up with increased lesson observations by the class teacher who realised that things were not getting any better. I just didn't know what to do.

Critical questions

»   Why do you think Cole reacted in this way?

»   How could Cole alleviate his situation?

»   What single piece of action could Cole have taken to improve his situation?

»   If presented with a similar situation, what piece of advice would you give and what action would you take?

Evidently Cole was struggling to manage juggling his responsibilities as a parent alongside his commitments and responsibilities to his class and his role as a teacher. As a teacher, you are charged with being professional at all times. In fact, as you know, teachers at any stage in their career are expected to meet Part Two of the Teachers' Standards (DfE, 2011) related to professionalism. Often this is interpreted by NQTs to mean that information shared with colleagues (especially their induction mentor) is purely on a work level and should not contain the personal. But think again about this perspective to professionalism. Was Cole being professional in terms of pupils accessing an engaging curriculum? Were the pupils learning in his lessons? Was he fulfilling the contractual and wider responsibilities of a teacher? It is evident from Cole's account that the answer to all these questions is no. Therefore, Cole could not demonstrate that he was meeting Part Two of the Teachers' Standards.

If you take nothing else from Cole's situation, then take this one piece of advice. Let your induction mentor know that something is wrong as soon as possible. They are there to support you and can make suggestions as to what aspects of your teaching can be relaxed. It is certainly better for them to know your situation. If you cannot tell the induction mentor, then find someone else on the staff that you can confide in.

Sources of support

NQT support networks

You will have access to a range of support networks as an NQT. These networks are important not just in times of trouble but also for sharing best practice.

Your appropriate body can provide support, along with other colleagues in your school including your induction mentor. Furthermore, your union may have designated support for NQTs so do take time to investigate this. There are also a number of websites that provide additional information for NQTs along with ideas for lessons etc. Sites include the University of Worcester's NQT Pinterest site, which is free and open to all, and the University of Derby's NQT web resources. You can find further information about these sites in the Further Reading section below.

TeachMeets and other networks

TeachMeets are informal events, often organised by a school, training provider or other educational body to enable teachers to share ideas. They generally centre on a theme, with brief presentations linked explicitly to classroom practice. Powerpoints are frowned upon and presentations are generally about six to eight minutes long. There is plenty of opportunity for discussion and idea-sharing in a way not always possible at a full conference. Website details are listed in the Further Reading section.

Twitter is a social network forum that can be used for professional networking, although it is strongly advised you do not use a personal account for your professional purpose. Setting up a Twitter account purely for following and contributing to professional debate will allow you to access current thinking and interact with educationalists in real time. LinkedIn is another online forum, primarily for professional networking across all sectors.

Supporting your subject knowledge and pedagogy

When you are faced with a class of pupils one major concern for you as an NQT is to find quality resources and ideas for promoting outstanding teaching and learning. One such set of resources can be accessed through the science, technology, engineering and mathematics organisation (STEM; see www.nationalstemcentre.org.uk/home) whose role is to promote both quality teaching and teachers' subject knowledge. STEM will provide you with resources and a curriculum framework enabling progression and interest in the STEM subjects. Through their e-library (www.nationalstemcentre.org.uk/resources) you will be able to access resource packs to support the teaching of particular topics. There are also resource groups that identify innovative new materials and ideas that you can use in your teaching. Additionally, you may also want to consult MESH (www.meshguides.org) which provides teachers and other educators with quick access to summaries of research-based specialist knowledge to support their professional judgement.

Meeting parents

There is considerable literature around the benefits of positive engagement with parents in a child's education (DCSF, 2008). For you, one of the most daunting moments in the autumn term will come with your first parents' evening, which will generally take the form of a 'meet and greet' some time before the October half-term. This is a formal opportunity for you to discuss how the pupils in your class have settled into their new learning environment, how they are reacting to you and how at this early stage they are progressing both academically and socially.

This meeting should not, however, be an opportunity for you to present parents with a stored-up bank of concerns regarding a child in your class since these should have already been addressed by you via the day-to-day contact you have with your parents. Instead, it should be a continuation of the process of you getting to know and share information with parents about pupils. It should be used to build up a mutual understanding of how you can work together to support their child during the coming year. Some schools have a policy that on this occasion, since pupils may have produced relatively little evidence of their learning, books should not be made readily available for parents to look at. However, it is important for you to have them to hand in case the need arises (through your discussion) and you wish to illustrate your point with evidence.

Booking appointments

The first hurdle you may face with parents' evening is booking an appropriate timeslot for each set of parents. Though schools will issue a standard letter on all teachers' behalf outlining the format and timings for this event, you may find that booking appointments is sometimes handled centrally by the administrator/school secretary or sometimes by yourself. If bookings are handled by someone other than yourself, remember the following points.

CHECKLIST

Booking parents' evening appointments

✓   Block out slots to give you a comfort break between groups of appointments or to allow you to catch up due to overrunning appointments.

✓   Since early and late appointments will be popular, avoid the temptation of fitting an extra slot in to please a parent.

✓   If a child in your class has a sibling, liaise with other teachers regarding their appointment times to avoid clashes or long waits for parents.

✓   If you know a particular parent may need extra time, book them where you have gaps either side of their appointment.

✓   Remember to confirm the times with parents using reply slips.

Parents' evenings

On the day make certain your room is tidy and that you have arranged seating where you want parents to wait. Place a timetable of the appointments on your door so parents can see how they fit into the timings of the event as a whole. Some schools operate a 'knock on the door' policy by parents when their time slots have arrived to help you keep to timings. If this is not the case keep your eye on the clock but do not appear rude by rushing parents if their time has elapsed. If you do find that a topic is too big for the time allocated, always suggest they make a separate appointment for it to be discussed properly.

Consider Geena's feelings about her first parents' evening detailed below, and reflect on what should be done to address her worries.

CASE STUDY

Geena's experience

I was really nervous meeting Mr and Mrs Dix. Although I have met mum, I had not really talked to dad before. I was worried I would not say the right things or say too little or too much about Lucy. I was really worried that they were going to ask me how she was doing compared to her best friend. I was also worried how I might broach the issue of her seeming lack of confidence in answering questions in class.

Critical questions

»   *What might Geena have said to start the conversation?*

»   *What sort of impression did Geena need to create?*

»   *What other information should Geena have had to hand?*

It is important you talk to your mentor about any concerns you have about parents' evenings. They will probably know the parents and will remember how you must be feeling. They will be able to help you with ideas about dealing with difficult parents or situations that might arise. They may even offer to come and sit with you through the more difficult appointments to provide reassurance. Also, if there are any parents you feel particularly nervous about dealing with, do mention this to the headteacher who may arrange to drop into this meeting just to see how things are going and stay and support you if necessary.

You, like Geena, need to remember that parents are attending this event not only to find out about their child but also to see and understand the teacher that their child talks about when they return from school. Start with a positive statement such as 'what a delightful child they have' but ground it in reality mentioning things they know to be true about their child. Above all they will be looking for someone who is truthful but also someone who is caring and wishes to support the development of their child as a 'whole'. Since you will have already built up a rapport with those parents you have talked to on a regular basis, use this ongoing knowledge of their lives to start the conversation as an ice breaker, for example, 'how did you get on last week at the vets?'

Parents will want to know about how their child is progressing and behaving. If you are asked to compare their child with another, politely remind them that you are not able to discuss other children with them. It is important that you are prepared for any questions regarding progress by having access to pupil records, test marks and children's books so you can answer their questions as fully as possible. Also have your diary available should you need to make a further appointment to continue a discussion.

Remember the parents will know more about their child than you do so ask them what they are like at home. For example, do your impressions of them being shy match what they are like at home? Is there anything the parents do that has a particular benefit in helping their child to be more confident? If so, discuss how you (and they) can encourage the pupil to take a more active role in lessons and to be more confident in front of others. Make certain you build in a review date so that you can touch base with either or both of the parents regarding the progress that has been made with any issues that have been identified as a result of your discussion.

Seeking further advice

If there are any issues discussed during the meeting with parents that you feel are outside your area of expertise or class-based responsibilities, for example, a parent wishing to have their child tested for dyslexia, signpost them to the appropriate professional – in this case, the SENCO (Special Educational Needs Co-ordinator). Make sure that you assure them that you will also follow this up on their behalf and that you will communicate the result of this meeting with them.

Remember you are new to the school and as such you may not have all the answers or knowledge to deal with detailed questions about policy or historic happenings. If you feel you are unable to make an honest and correct comment, do not commit yourself at this moment. Use a delay tactic such as 'oh I am sorry but I have not come across this aspect of school so far and will check with the headteacher'. Tell them you will do so preferably after the appointment is over. After you have checked out the query arrange to give feedback to the parents as soon as is practical. Start by saying 'I have now had chance to ask the headteacher and ...'.

After parents' evening is over find time to talk to other staff about any experiences and issues you might have had. If a parent concerned you, find out how staff dealt with them in the past or if they have experienced something similar. This will help you build up your bank of ideas and responses ready for your next meeting.

CHECKLIST

Parents' evening tips

✓ Speak clearly and maintain eye contact.

✓ Do not interrupt, no matter how pressing you feel your point is.

✓ Jot down anything you want to raise if a speaker has yet to finish.

✓ Listen to what is being said rather than half-listening because you might be mentally rehearsing your point.

✓ Make clear statements using a few well-chosen facts.

✓ Be succinct so others will stay focused on your point.

✓ Believe in what you say since it shows commitment.

Other school-based meetings

Staff meetings are an important and useful professional development opportunity as well as providing a chance to outline operational issues to do with the school's day-to-day running.

The first major meeting you will attend is the professional development day. This tends to be arranged for the day prior to the start of each term depending on how the term dates work out. Sometimes they may be split into two half-day sessions, which are commonly known as twilights. If twilights are used they will normally follow on from a teaching day sometime in the term. There are contractually five professional development days, which each complement other staff meetings that fall under the directed time element of your contractual requirement. Attendance at both professional development days and staff meetings is compulsory. However, for part-time employees, this will be pro rata.

Professional development days

The agendas for professional development days will usually depend on the time of year. Therefore, the first day will usually be linked to items associated with the coming year, while the last day will focus on preparing for the following year. Generally, the middle three are dedicated to staff development training linked to topical issues or items linked to developments that can improve teaching and learning. Sometimes all teaching and non-teaching staff will be required to attend if the items involve training linked to whole school issues, while at other times just teaching staff will be required to attend.

Your first professional development day is important because it provides an opportunity for you to see the dynamics within your new team. Who appears to dominate discussion? Who is confrontational, and who says very little? This first event is usually a social occasion, a chance for individuals to catch up on summer news and to establish the goals for the coming year. Usually a shared lunch will have been organised to lighten the mood and facilitate staff discussion and collegiality. Make certain you try and sit by someone who you feel will help you feel comfortable during this meeting such as your induction mentor.

You will always know the format of the coming day since an agenda will have been circulated in advance. Sometimes this first event will involve an outside speaker, sometimes other neighbouring schools may be invited to attend or it may just focus on a curriculum focus led by key staff such as the literacy co-ordinator. For some schools it will involve half the day spent in the meeting and the other half given over to preparations and discussion between the year co-ordinators and their staff. Make sure you have your diary with you since some schools will even use part of the day to discuss duty rotas, hall timetabling or concert dates.

Usually you won't be required to say much at a professional development day so it is an opportunity for you to listen and observe and start to consider what contribution you can make to any discussion. Sometimes the day has an active focus, for example, if drama is a developmental area. If you feel you can offer any insights or opinions linked to the topic under discussion, join in since one of the reasons you were appointed was for the fresh and new dynamics you can bring to the existing team. Do not be afraid to ask about anything you do not understand even if it is to your mentor later in the day. Remember no one will be expecting you to know the nuances of all that has been discussed and they will be more than happy to help you at the start of your new career. You can expect that someone may note that your idea has been tried before but that does not mean that it should be dismissed. Clearly articulate the value of what you are suggesting; this may lead to your idea being reconsidered despite initial scepticism.

Staff meetings

These meetings will feel more formal compared to the professional development days. Again there will be an agenda that will be circulated prior to the event and normally the overview for the term's meetings will also be made available in advance.

The majority of staff meeting time will be related to teaching and learning matters. There will be times when they primarily disseminate information regarding policy and procedure such as a new policy or changes to a tracking system. At other times they will provide a sounding board for future plans or discussion related to alterations of policy. Whatever they are used for, remember you have a role to play and an opinion to share.

If you feel really strongly about anything that is raised in a staff meeting and you feel it might come across inappropriately, remember you do not always have to respond during the meeting. You can always go and see the person after the meeting and privately air your difference of opinion or concerns. This can sometimes be the best option for you or others to avoid losing face.

Pupil progress meetings

As part of a school's drive to improve standards and whole school improvement you will be invited to attend a pupil review meeting during the middle of the autumn term. This will then be followed by review meetings in the spring and summer terms. Your mentor will no doubt have made you aware of the purpose of such meetings. This could include the need for you to identify pupils whose progress has been above or below what is expected. Although attainment levels have been removed by the government, many schools continue to operate this system as teachers and parents are all familiar with it. Each school will have the flexibility in future to use a system that they prefer; however, the following has been included as a point of reference. Remember normally a school would expect pupils to have made the minimum progress of two national curriculum levels or twelve Average Points across each key stage. For Key Stage 1 this will mean one sublevel or two Average Points Scores (APS) per term, one level 6 APS each year, or two levels or twelve APS in two years. For Key Stage 2 this will involve one APS each term, three APS per year, one level or six APS in two years, or two levels/twelve APS in four years.

Pupil progress meetings will also be used to support school leaders in understanding why identified pupils have made the progress they have. These meetings also help them target future interventions to benefit not only individual pupils but also to support progress across the entire cohort in a particular subject. It can allow them to identify trends and common themes, for example, progress by boys in writing, and such information can be used to support future staff development.

Peter has been invited to attend his first progress meeting. He is worried that the meeting might focus on his abilities as a trainee teacher. Consider how he might best prepare for such a meeting.

CASE STUDY

Peter's experience

I was really worried that my headteacher was going to start asking me why I had not done anything to help the pupils in my class who had not made any progress. I was worried he would not understand that I am trying my best but there are so many other pupils to support in my class. I am working really hard but whatever I do does not seem to have any impact upon their progress.

Critical questions

»   *Who might Peter have talked to in order to best prepare him for this meeting?*

»   *What information should Peter have considered before going into the meeting?*

To prepare for such a meeting you, like Peter, should talk to your induction mentor so that you understand that the meeting is not really directed at an individual's quality of teaching. You will have already been observed teaching and this is when you will be given feedback about the quality of your teaching and how it may be developed. The pupil progress meeting is about identifying those pupils who despite your and perhaps others' best efforts have failed to make the anticipated progress. It is also about celebrating those individuals who have made above average progress and identifying why they have done particularly well. This in turn may give clues to how others might be helped in class to make similar gains.

To prepare for the meeting you really need to look at the pupil tracking systems in your school before the meeting commences to identify which pupils are likely to be discussed. Try to think about and identify if there is any particular reason for the rates of progress identified. Is slow progress due to a pastoral issue such as mum being ill or dad being out of the country? Consider how interventions have been implemented for any identified pupils and if they have led to any particular results. Also, have learning conversations with pupils given you any insights into their levels of progress such as what have they found difficult and why? What could help them in the future?

Remember for some pupils it will be about making small incremental gains in terms of their progress. These progress meetings are part of the school trying to make subtle adaptations to teaching and learning so that marginal gains can be made and so that the provision provided is mapped appropriately to maximise progress.

CHECKLIST

Progress

✓   Which individuals have made better than expected progress? Can you identify why this is so?

✓   Which pupils appear to have made little if any progress? Can you identify why this is so?

✓   Can class-based provision be adapted to help support pupil progress?

✓   Would additional targeted support help their progress?

✓   Are there any trends across literacy and numeracy worth noting?

✓   Is there any support or training that could help you improve pupil progress?

Further reading

Department for Education (DfE) (no date) *Get into Teaching*. [online] Available at: www.education.gov.uk/get-into-teaching/about-teaching/induction-year (accessed 29 November 2015).

Department for Education (DfE) (2011) *Teachers' Standards: Guidance for School Leaders, School Staff and Governing Bodies*. London: HMSO.

Department for Education (DfE) (2015) *Induction for Newly Qualified Teachers (England): Statutory Guidance for Appropriate Bodies, Headteachers, School Staff and Governing Bodies*. [online] Available at: www.gov.uk/government/uploads/system/uploads/attachment_data/file/458233/Statutory_induction_guidance_for_newly_qualified_teachers.pdf (accessed 29 November 2015).

TeachMeet (no date) *Teachers Sharing Ideas with Teachers: Front Page*. [online] Available at: http://teachmeet.pbworks.com/w/page/19975349/FrontPage (accessed 29 November 2015).

University of Derby (no date) *NQT Support*. [online] Available at: www.derby.ac.uk/education/nqt-support/ (accessed 8 December 2015).

University of Worcester (no date) *Primary NQT Pinterest* [online] Available at: www.worcester.ac.uk/discover/primary-nqt-pinterest.html (accessed 29 November 2015).

3 Second term: getting into your stride

TIMELINE

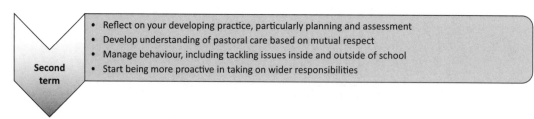

| Second term | • Reflect on your developing practice, particularly planning and assessment
• Develop understanding of pastoral care based on mutual respect
• Manage behaviour, including tackling issues inside and outside of school
• Start being more proactive in taking on wider responsibilities |

Teachers' Standards

The following Teachers' Standards (DfE, 2011) are applicable to this chapter.

2.   *Promote good progress and outcomes by pupils*

   • *be accountable for pupils' attainment, progress and outcomes*

7. *Manage behaviour effectively to ensure a good and safe learning environment*

- *have clear rules and routines for behaviour in classrooms, and take responsibility for promoting good and courteous behaviour both in classrooms and around the school, in accordance with the school's behaviour policy*

- *have high expectations of behaviour, and establish a framework for discipline with a range of strategies, using praise, sanctions and rewards consistently and fairly*

- *manage classes effectively, using approaches which are appropriate to pupils' needs in order to involve and motivate them*

- *maintain good relationships with pupils, exercise appropriate authority, and act decisively when necessary.*

8. *Fulfil wider professional responsibilities*

- *make a positive contribution to the wider life and ethos of the school*

- *develop effective professional relationships with colleagues, knowing how and when to draw on advice and specialist support*

- *deploy support staff effectively*

- *take responsibility for improving teaching through appropriate professional development, responding to advice and feedback from colleagues*

- *communicate effectively with parents with regard to pupils' achievements and well-being*

Time to reflect: planning and assessment

Teachers are accountable for pupils' attainment, progress and outcomes, not only in terms of the Teachers' Standards (DfE, 2011) but because this is central to the teaching role. At this point in your NQT year you may be more confident in responding to pupils' needs and planning for progression but it doesn't hurt to reflect on how long-term planning, embedded formative assessment and meaningful baseline and summative assessment will help you.

The removal of the single system of ongoing assessment (in the form of level descriptors linked to the national curriculum, 1998) has meant schools are now able to select their own assessment system. This means that you may not have developed experience of using your school's assessment processes during your training, which could leave you feeling very uncertain about what is expected.

The 2013 consultation into Primary Assessment and Accountability identified core principles for effective assessment, which are shown in Figure 3.1. Whatever system is being used in your setting should be underpinned by these principles.

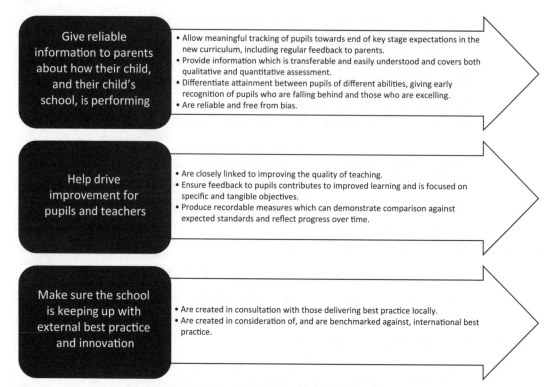

Figure 3.1 *Assessment principles: effective assessment (DfE, 2014c)*

CASE STUDY

Maya's experience

I have just finished my first term as an NQT and I can honestly say that I am even more con-fused about assessment than I was before. I expected my mentor to model how to use the school's assessment system for me but this hasn't happened. If I am honest, I have had no support at all. I have had to work it out myself. Luckily I have been able to ask the NQT from last year, who is good with the online pupil tracker we use. Everything I know I learnt through my chats with her or worked it out for myself. But now I am worried my assessments may not be accurate because I have been left on my own all term in everything! All our assessment is done online, so all assessment discussion/training has been through using the tracker.

Critical questions

»   *How could Maya have used the assessment principles in Figure 3.1 to help her be more secure in her judgements?*

»   *What CPD could she request as part of her NQT allocation?*

»   *How could moderation support her development and who should be involved? Consider mentoring, other staff, etc*

While online and other tracker systems can be useful in recording progress, being able to input the data should not be mistaken for a detailed understanding of how to assess. There are two key points regarding effective assessment that might help Maya:

1.   Differentiate attainment between pupils of different abilities, giving early recognition of pupils who are falling behind and those who are excelling.

2.   Ensure pupils' feedback contributes to improved learning and is focused on specific and tangible objectives.

Both of these points explicitly involve the pupils' learning and require Maya to have secure subject knowledge to ensure appropriate curriculum coverage is linked to meaningful assessment opportunities. However, first of all Maya has to be clear about the different types of assessment she is expected to undertake and the different purpose of each one.

Wiliam (2004, p 1) identifies three broad functions of assessment as seen in Figure 3.2. Although this is often an integrated and cyclical process, Wiliam proposes (based on significant seminal research) that the formative function comes first.

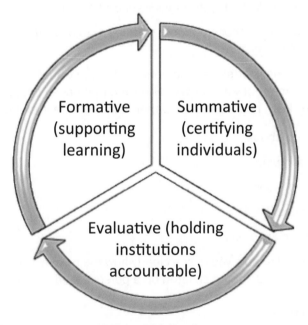

Figure 3.2 *Functions of assessment (Wiliam, 2004, p 1)*

Critical questions

»   *What is the role of formative assessment in your classroom?*

»   *Can a single assessment be used formatively and for summative purposes or do you need to plan for different discrete assessment opportunities? Explain your answer.*

Wiliam (2004) discusses the way that the term *formative assessment* is often used inter-changeably with *assessment for learning*, which can complicate the matter. However, he defines formative assessment as being a function, designed to inform and alter the intended teaching, while assessment for learning is a process which focuses on helping the learner progress. For example, peer feedback may be acted upon by pupils to make changes to their output or to aid their understanding. But it only becomes formative if the teacher then uses it to adapt his or her teaching to meet the learning needs of the pupils, ie changes the task in light of the assessment. Thus, the function of true formative assessment is to inform your planning.

Making the most of the assessment collated in lessons

In order to make a meaningful link between planning and assessment you need to be able to reflect on the data you have collected. This requires effective record keeping that is easy to access and use. While summative and evaluative data may be available on pupil-trackers, some of the formative data may be more temporal and difficult to evidence.

Critical questions

» *What records do you keep as part of your general classroom practice?*

» *How do you pull together observations, marking data and other forms of assessment to create a formative picture?*

This sort of record keeping is often very personal to the individual teacher, and what works for other professionals may not work for you. However, that doesn't mean that it is not worth asking them how they keep records that help them plan. Different methods may include:

- a journal-style notebook;
- notes on a lesson plan;
- a published mark book;
- Excel spreadsheets;
- sticky notes in a plastic wallet.

The point is that it should enable you to see clearly how the next lesson needs to be adapted to address the learning needs of the children on a personalised or differentiated basis.

Working with others

It is also worth considering assessment and planning input from learning support assistants, both with regard to individual pupils and to the class as a whole. This may need to be built up over time, and will rely on clarity and rapport between you and your staff member(s). Megginson and Clutterbuck (2005, p 18) have characterised the effect of clarity and rapport in a mentoring context. Figure 3.3 provides a good framework for identifying issues and ways of working successfully with your support staff.

In order to use this framework, it is helpful to think about what behaviours are needed from both the teacher and support staff to encourage clarity and rapport.

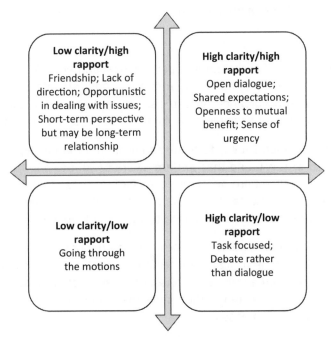

Figure 3.3 *A framework for working successfully with others (Megginson and Clutterbuck, 2005, p 18)*

Evaluative assessment: preparing for statutory standardised assessments

Currently there are several key assessment checkpoints for different aspects of the primary curriculum in England (see Figure 3.4).

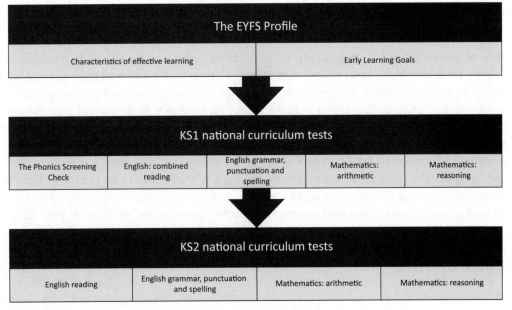

Figure 3.4 *Statutory standardised assessments in England*

Each checkpoint has a set of assessment reporting arrangements (ARAs) which headteachers and local authority assessment co-ordinators use to ensure the process is fair nationally. Current arrangements and guidance around assessment are produced by the Standards and Testing Agency (www.gov.uk/government/organisations/standards-and-testing-agency).

It is the headteacher's responsibility to ensure that all information regarding the statutory procedures is shared with you and that you are aware of your role in the administration of such tests. If you are at all unsure or require clarification you should ask your headteacher in the first instance, but an awareness of the documentation can be useful. The ARAs are produced in a handbook that can be accessed using the link above.

Key to the successful administration of these tests is adequate preparation. Ensuring any necessary spare equipment is available for tests is essential: some schools prepare trays with all the necessary equipment for each class. Children need to understand how the process will work and what is expected of them in terms of behaviour, so think about how you can familiarise them with the process.

Preparing children does not mean teaching to the test for the term leading up to it, however. Although test conditions do need to be rehearsed in order to establish the most effective way of using the time, a constant regime of testing without appropriate learning and teaching will not help attainment or progress.

Baseline assessment

Because of the processes outlined above you are likely to have information about the majority of your pupils prior to the beginning of the year. Occasionally you will have new entrants to your class who have no documentation, for example, asylum seekers or Looked After Children who have been moved from their homes as an emergency measure. Therefore, it is useful to consider how you can gather baseline assessment data that will enable you to teach them appropriately as quickly as possible.

Where schools have a full programme of summative assessments linked to pupil-trackers it may be possible to use the previous assessment taken by the class to gain a snapshot of where the pupil currently is. However, be aware that the test is likely to have key gaps if it is part of a wider scheme. It is worth thinking about your current teaching but also the wider expectations regarding national curriculum attainment appropriate to the year and devising a series of opportunities for the pupil to demonstrate their knowledge and understanding. The National Foundation for Educational Research in England and Wales and other similar organisations have produced suites of tests to support analysis of pupil progress. However, it would be beneficial for you to develop your own assessment literacy in order to feel confident that you can design your own assessments when appropriate: see the Further Reading section for helpful texts to support this.

Pastoral care

As a class teacher you now have direct responsibility for the pastoral support of the children in your care. It is vital that you develop good relationships with the children's parents so that you feel informed should issues arise and so that you know how best to approach them. This relationship must involve you constantly engaging with parents and taking the time to listen to them.

Communication is the key to your success, whether it is through more formal means such as parents' evenings or through informal discussions at the end of the school day. Remember you should invest time in the children's parents before it is needed. This will lead to the use of the most effective approach should you need to engage with parents at a later date. However, despite your best efforts pastoral issues will arise and these might include:

* poor attendance;

* non-collection at the end of the school day;

* the need to restrain pupils for their own and others' safety;

* child protection and pupil safety issues;

* supporting and signposting parents or guardians for support both within the school and the wider educational community.

Attendance

During your NQT year you will have realised that one of the greatest barriers linked to pupil progress is that of attendance. As the DfE (2014e, p 4) attendance guidance notes:

> Missing out on lessons leaves children vulnerable to falling behind. Children with poor attendance tend to achieve less in both primary and secondary school.

Since school attendance is statutory, your school is required by law to follow strict advice (DfE, 2014e) and guidance and to have a clear policy relating to attendance. Your school will require you to register, either electronically or manually, twice a day if a child is present in your class. If a child is out of school for exceptional reasons such as illness, medicals, approved holidays or educational visits then additional codes in the register will be needed to signify this. However, if a child fails to attend school it will normally be your job to ascertain the reason for a child's absence. In the majority of cases either the school office or you will have been notified by letter or phone call about a required absence. If this is the case you will record the absence as authorised using the appropriate code. However, if in consultation with other more senior colleagues no reasonable reason can be given for an absence then you may be required to record it as an unauthorised absence, which means this absence is not approved by the school. Remember the school will not condone unauthorised absence so if this continues your line managers will have to liaise with the school mentor or the council's educational welfare officer to see if the situation can be improved. It may be that safeguarding actions have been taken and if all this does not resolve the issue then the process may ultimately lead to parental prosecution.

CASE STUDY

Sian's experience

I was worried when Simon did not come into class one morning. He was a happy little boy who was always on time and looked ready for school. His mum usually dropped him off in the playground and I had not seen him this morning. His mum always contacted the school to inform us if Simon was absent so it was very unusual and it was playing on my mind as I knew how conscientious the family were about Simon's attendance at school.

Critical questions

»　　*How could Sian have found out the reason for Simon's absence?*

»　　*Is Sian's knowledge of the parent important in this scenario?*

Firstly, Sian must contact the office to check whether a reason has been given for Simon's absence. If this is the case she will be advised which absence code to use. Sian could also ask the children if Simon had been seen in the playground without worrying them. She should however remember this is not the most reliable source of information to base her actions on. Given her knowledge of Simon and his mum it could be that she should be less worried than if another child was absent whom, for example, is known to be at risk.

If no reason can be ascertained for the absence it will then fall to the named school attendance officer to contact home or the parent(s) to see where Simon is. If no reason can be found for the absence this could be escalated to a child protection issue.

Pupil collection

Each school will have a particular way in which they wish you to dismiss pupils at the end of the school day, but as a general rule the younger the pupils the greater the need to hand them over personally to a responsible adult. It is important that you start to recognise the relationships children have with those who generally collect them. If you see someone who you do not recognise coming to pick up a child ask the child who they are so you know that the child is happy to go with them. If the child is of little help you will no doubt wish to be certain of their well-being in releasing the child to that other person's care. In these circumstances it is prudent to check with the parent via their preferred contact details before releasing the child. If a child is at risk some schools ask unfamiliar adults to give you a special security word before you are allowed to release the child to their care. If this is the case you will be told this well in advance. Remember since you are acting 'in loco parentis', if children are not collected by a responsible adult you have responsibility for that child until they are collected. Therefore, if a child is not collected you will be responsible for them until you follow school procedure to hand them over to another adult. This may mean them waiting with the school secretary or even the headteacher until they are finally collected.

Behaviour and discipline

Effective behaviour management is a key government national priority and is explicitly inspected by Ofsted. The government clearly outlines what is expected of school staff in terms of managing behaviour and discipline (DfE, 2014d) both inside and outside of the school context. You should therefore ensure that you have read and understood the school behaviour policy. There are many strategies that you can employ to manage behaviour but remember you cannot be effective in this area in isolation. There needs to be a consistent approach across the school so that all pupils appreciate the expectations placed upon them and that there is consistency among staff.

You will probably have some experience of low-level disruption. Defining low-level disruption is problematic as what might be deemed as low-level by one individual may not be regarded as such by another colleague. For the purposes of this book, however, we refer to low-level disruption as those behaviours that are not confrontational or challenging but do disturb your teaching and pupils' learning. Often this is through pupils moving around the class when they should be sitting and listening (movement), wasting time (time) and/or mutterings and whisperings between pupils (talk).

In high-level disruption the misconduct is overtly confrontational, hostile, provocative and challenging. Pupils may blatantly challenge your authority, refuse to obey the class/school rules and even deliver verbal or physical abuse to pupils, or responsible adults. While thankfully these situations are rare, you may be working in a school in challenging circumstances or have a pupil in your class that has specific needs and who may be volatile due to a whole host of reasons. Trying to manage high-level disruption is arduous and exhausting over a sustained period of time and can be detrimental to your health and well-being. See Chapter 5 for further information on how to look after your health and well-being.

Clearly you need to have strategies in place to deal with the range of behaviour issues that you may encounter in your NQT period. Before you decide on the strategies you might employ to improve behaviour in your classroom, consider how you react to the different categories and forms of behaviour currently evident in your classroom. Managing behaviour in your classroom means more than just responding to unsuitable conduct; it is about constructing an environment that encourages positive behaviour.

Critical questions

» *Using the table below, tick all of the statements that apply to you when dealing with behaviour in your class.*

» *Try to think about both low- and high-level disruption and consider whether you react differently based on the various forms of poor behaviour.*

Table 3.1 *Personal reactions to behavioural incidents*

REACTION	✔
stay calm	
pretend I have not heard or seen anything	
fail to react	
reactive rather than proactive	
overreact	
use pupil restraining techniques	
argue	
get angry	
use a behaviour/discipline plan	
become hostile	
follow the behaviour policy and guidance	
threaten actions but not follow through	
respond proportionately	
scream, shout or cry	
make sarcastic comments	
leave the classroom	
make unkind comments	
send the pupil from the classroom	
laugh	
behave inconsistently and unfairly	
use sanctions	
call or send for another member of staff or headteacher	
use a planned, well-established and consistent approach	

Setting classroom rules

From the outset you should ensure that you set your parameters and your expectations of the pupils with the class by designing a set of classroom rules, as mentioned in Chapter 1. Unless you trained through a school provider, you may not have previously witnessed a class teacher conducting this crucial activity. If you get this right from the outset, your job of managing the class and creating a learning environment will be made easier. Classroom rules should fit with your school's rules and ethos, and ideally they should be negotiated with your pupils. The following top five tips should help you improve how you set rules and procedures in your class.

1.   Create positive rules; not a list of do nots.

2.   Negotiate and compromise with pupils so that there is a sense of ownership among the class.

3.   Get the pupils to make rule posters and display these.

4.   Review the class rules with the class on a regular basis, particularly if you have a lesson that could result in poor behaviour (eg use of musical instruments) or if you have a hunch that something is not quite right.

5.   Encourage pupils to self-assess themselves against the rules.

In order to enforce your class rules you will need to think about a range of rewards and sanctions, again ensuring that these fit with your school's behaviour policy.

Use of force and restraining pupils

Sometime in your career you may find that you are required in some way to restrain or protect a child from another's actions or from hurting themselves. Though there may be a designated person who should be called should this happen, in all probability you will find that immediate action is required for you to secure all pupils' safety. In such situations you should be aware that your school will have its own policy linked to government guidance on the use of 'reasonable force', often found in the school's behaviour policy. Reasonable force is deemed to mean that you will be required to use 'no more force than is needed' (DfE, 2013b, p 4). Should it be likely that you will need to use reasonable force with a child, most schools will give relevant training to minimise you harming a child or yourself. Such training may form part of the induction package offered by your school.

Behaviour outside school

The DfE (2014d) guidance clearly states under which circumstances poor pupil behaviour outside school can be addressed. Using Rachel's situation below, consider whether you are allowed to deal with this set of circumstances based on the law and your school context (eg academy, independent, maintained etc). You may want to refer to the guidance in order to make your decisions.

CASE STUDY

Rachel's experience

I had finished teaching for the day and had sent my Year 6 class home with their parents/carers. Some of the parents permit their child to walk or cycle alone because they are in their final year of primary school. On this day, however, it wasn't long before I received a phone call from one of the parents. They had witnessed Joey (a child who walks on his own to and from school) picking up stones and throwing them at cats, front doors, wheels of cars and missing passers-by through the narrowest of margins. Joey was often getting into scrapes at school and was quite physical with the other boys so I wasn't surprised to hear of his antics on his way home. I wasn't sure whether I could tackle Joey about his behaviour and didn't know what to do.

Critical questions

» *If you found yourself in Rachel's situation, what would you do?*

» *Who would you speak to?*

» *Is there any further information you would need?*

» *According to the law, can you tackle Joey's behaviour?*

» *What sanctions would you impose that are proportionate to his misconduct?*

In the first instance you would be well advised to discuss the incident with your induction mentor or headteacher in addition to consulting with the school behaviour policy. Make sure you make a note of the time you received the phone call and the name of the parent who expressed concerns. While talking to the parent or other confidante, you may also want to ask if anyone else witnessed Joey's actions. The DfE (2014d, p 9) guidance is unambiguous and explicitly states that misbehaviour out of school can be tackled by teachers when the pupil is:

• taking part in any school-organised or school-related activity;

• travelling to or from school;

• wearing school uniform;

• in some other way identifiable as a pupil at the school.

In addition, misbehaviour at any time can be tackled, whether or not the conditions above apply, if it:

• could have repercussions for the orderly running of the school or;

• poses a threat to another pupil or member of the public or;

• could adversely affect the reputation of the school.

Dealing with bullying

With the advance of digital technology, forms of bullying go beyond those of physical aggression and increasingly invade what would have been regarded as private spaces of sanctuary, for example, the pupil's home. Your school may have a separate anti-bullying policy; if so ensure that you are familiar with it. You may also have a racial equality policy and inclusion policy, all of which you should be conversant with so that you can deal with a range of bullying issues should they present themselves. Bullying occurs in all walks of life and within differing types of school, including primary.

Critical questions

» *How would you define bullying?*

» *What forms of bullying are you aware of?*

» *What strategies do you have in place for dealing with bullying?*

Your school should have its own definition of bullying. However, the DfE (2015b) defines bullying as behaviour that is:

* *repeated;*

* *intended to hurt someone either physically or emotionally;*

* *often aimed at specific groups, eg because of race, religion, gender or sexual orientation.*

Bullying takes many forms and includes teasing, name calling, making threats, physical assault and more recently cyberbullying. Cyberbullying comprises bullying via mobile technologies such as a mobile phone or an iPad. It can be administered online through email, social media/networks and instant messaging. Many primary pupils now have a mobile phone and access to the internet at home. In order to combat bullying, you will want to establish transparency related to what constitutes bullying and discuss this with the pupils in your class. It is best to have a range of preventative strategies that you can deploy such as circle time, peer mediation and restorative justice (see Further Reading for more information).

Behaviour for Learning (B4L)

In order for pupils to learn, establishing good behaviour within your classroom is paramount. It is perceived that if the level of academic work is pitched well for all pupils, behaviour should reflect this and remain good. However, poor pupil behaviour is a barrier to learning effectively.

The Behaviour for Learning (B4L) website, now held in the National Archives (see Further Reading), determines three key relationships that influence pupils' ability to learn: the relationship with self, others and the curriculum, as outlined in Figure 3.5.

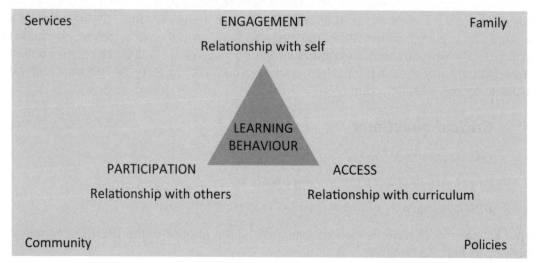

Figure 3.5 *Behaviour for Learning conceptual framework (based on the B4L diagram taken from EPPI review, 2004)*

With the B4L conceptual framework in mind, read Deena's account of the behavioural situation she faced.

CASE STUDY

Deena's classroom behaviour incident

I knew I was in for a day of it as soon as Darius arrived at school that morning. On greeting him in the playground his face was like thunder and when I enquired as to how he was feeling it was evident that things were not right. He angrily stated that he'd had a bad night with no tea because his mum didn't have enough money to buy any food. He had spent some of the night sitting on the porch having climbed out of his bedroom window so was tired and hungry. On entering the cloakroom, he hurled his coat across the cloakroom and shoved a few of the other children out of the way before storming into the classroom. I told Darius that we were going to be having English first and that we would be looking at a Jacqueline Wilson book so that he knew what to expect. Darius's perception of himself as a learner is poor and he always struggles in class with every area of the curriculum but particularly English.

Once in the classroom he sat with his head in his hands, kicking the chair legs but at least he was not hurting anyone else. I took the register and then moved the class to the carpet in order to start our first lesson (English). This resulted in some disruption from Darius as he noisily pushed his table and chair away in order to move to the carpet, finding a gap on the carpet at the back of the class. Throughout my teaching input Darius shouted out, pushed other children in the back while sitting on the carpet and generally made a nuisance of himself. I was beginning to lose my patience having ignored some of the initial behaviour. The last straw was when Darius swore at one of the children. I stopped my teaching and confronted Darius. It was like lighting touch paper! Darius reacted violently, grabbing a chair and flinging it across the classroom. I was terrified for the safety of the other pupils ultimately and myself. Darius then moved to find another chair and once more launched it into the ether. There was no abating his vehement behaviour and I was really unsure about what to do having never been presented with such an aggressive form of disruption previously.

Critical questions

» *Using the B4L conceptual framework, which aspects are not effectively catered for?*

» *What intervention strategies would you adopt if confronted with Deena's situation?*

» *What would you have done differently?*

» *Besides the behavioural issues, what other issues can you identify?*

» *Given the nature of Darius's background, who else would you talk to?*

Darius's situation is complex. Not only does he present behavioural concerns, his situation also relates to safeguarding and child protection. With the B4L conceptual framework in mind you might have identified the following areas that need further consideration for Darius to thrive in his learning behaviour. His own self-esteem and confidence to learn is low as Deena states that he struggles with all areas of the curriculum.

Clearly his family situation is impacting on Darius's ability to learn effectively given that he has not had adequate food and rest. Deena should pass this information on to the Designated Safeguarding Officer (DSO) at the school and keep a record of it herself so as to build a picture should the same thing happen again. Rather than taking Darius into class, Deena could have found some fruit and a quiet place for Darius to sit and eat something. In addition, finding an adult (preferably the person responsible for safeguarding) to discuss Darius's situation outside of the classroom would have helped to defuse the situation. It may also be the fact that social services are already involved with the family and Deena might take steps to check this through the DSO.

Due to his tendency to antagonise other pupils in his class by pushing, prodding and swearing, it can be assumed that Darius has dubious relationships with his classmates. Additionally, the choice of text for the lesson would not have been particularly appealing to Darius due to the gender bias towards girls. You should seriously consider the types of text and gender-specific bias they may have when selecting texts for your teaching.

Deena should have dealt with the immediacy of the behaviour from the outset. Having identified that Darius was upset, taking a positive and caring approach might have defused the situation. For example, she could have asked Darius to sit with her at the front of the carpet so that he could be her helper. Throughout the early stages of the misconduct Deena should follow the school behaviour policy and be consistent. With the advent of the violent behaviour Deena's priority is the safety of the rest of the pupils in her class. Rather than trying to restrain Darius, Deena should have removed the rest of her class from the classroom, shut the door on Darius and sent a pupil to the headteacher or deputy to ask for assistance.

CHECKLIST

Behaviour and discipline

✓ Read and familiarise yourself with the behaviour policy and any other associated policies, eg anti-bullying.

✓ Establish a clear set of class rules.

✓ Set the pitch of work for pupils appropriately through differentiated work.

Wider responsibilities

After settling in to your substantive teaching duties you will need to think about what involvement you will have with the wider school community and beyond. This is essential for you to be able to demonstrate your ability to address and evidence all of the Teachers' Standards (DfE, 2011) on the completion of your induction period. There are many opportunities available to you; however, you may want to explore new and creative alternatives to traditional engagement such as through international links.

You may be able to contribute to the wider development of the school and its involvement with the community in some of the following ways:

- run an extra-curricular club;

- organise a school trip;

- organise a charity fundraising event;

- contribute to a teacher training day or staff meeting;

- help organise and assist with sports days, fetes, Christmas fairs etc;

- arrange for an external speaker to come to the school;

- lead a whole school assembly for parents;

- be involved in school plays and performances;

- volunteer to assist with wrap around care, eg breakfast club.

You may wish to consider the possibility of extending an extra-curricular offer to the wider community, something that is becoming increasingly popular. Make sure that you have discussed this with your headteacher as there will be associated safeguarding considerations.

Often schools are involved in raising money for charity and you may have some connections with appropriate local causes. Throwing yourself into dressing up for good causes is all part and parcel of being a teacher so if you feel awkward about this aspect, then you will need to devise a strategy for dealing with this: for example, wear a mask as part of the costume so that you feel less conspicuous and self-conscious. Likewise, leading a celebration assembly for parents can often be daunting so you may want to consider working with a colleague in the first instance to deliver the assembly together or alternatively encourage your TA to take more of a central role.

Finally, in the role of class teacher you will be expected to work with other professionals from a range of disciplines, for example, health care professionals. This has increased in importance since the death of Victoria Climbie in 2000, Baby P in 2007 and Daniel Pelka in 2012. Multi-agency work, safeguarding and child protection are all dealt with in Chapter 4.

Further reading

Baginsky, W (2004) *Peer Mediation in the UK: A Guide for Schools*. [online] Available at: www.creducation. org/resources/peermediationintheuk.pdf (accessed 4 December 2015).

Behaviour 4 Learning (no date) *Positive Approaches in Behaviour Management*. [online] Available at: http://webarchive.nationalarchives.gov.uk/20101021152907/http:/www.behaviour4 learning.ac.uk/ViewArticle2.aspx?ContentId=13206 (accessed 5 December 2015).

Black, P, Harrison, C, Lee, C, Marshall, B and Wiliam, D (2002) *Working Inside the Black Box: Assessment for Learning in the Classroom*. London: Department of Education and Professional Studies, King's College London.

circle time (no date) *Releasing Excellence through Building Self-Esteem*. [online] Available at: www.circle-time.co.uk/ (accessed 4 December 2015).

Department for Education (DfE) (2013) *Preventing Bullying*. [online] Available at: www.gov.uk/ government/publications/preventing-and-tackling-bullying (accessed 4 December 2015).

Goswami, U (2015) *Children's Cognitive Development and Learning*. Cambridge Primary Review Trust/Pearson. [online] Available at: http://cprtrust.org.uk/research/learning/ (accessed 4 December 2015).

Harlen, W (2014) *Assessment, Standards and Quality of Learning in Primary Education*. Cambridge Primary Review Trust/Pearson. [online] Available at: http://cprtrust.org.uk/research/ assessment/ (accessed 4 December 2015).

Restorative Justice Council (no date) *Restorative Justice 4 Schools*. [online] Available at: www.restorativejustice4schools.co.uk/wp/?page_id=45 (accessed 4 December 2015).

4 Third term: the finish line is in sight

TIMELINE

Teachers' Standards

The following Teachers' Standards (DfE, 2011) are applicable to this chapter.

1. *Set high expectations which inspire, motivate and challenge pupils*

    *   *set goals that stretch and challenge pupils of all backgrounds, abilities and dispositions*

2. *Promote good progress and outcomes by pupils*

    *   *be accountable for pupils' attainment, progress and outcomes*

6. *Make accurate and productive use of assessment*

    *   *know and understand how to assess the relevant subject and curriculum areas, including statutory assessment requirements*

    *   *make use of formative and summative assessment to secure pupils' progress*

8. *Fulfil wider professional responsibilities*

    *   *develop effective professional relationships with colleagues, knowing how and when to draw on advice and specialist support*

    *   *deploy support staff effectively*

    *   *communicate effectively with parents with regard to pupils' achievements and well-being*

Introduction

This chapter highlights the need for you to form successful working relationships with outside agencies and support staff. It reviews your role in extra-curricular activities, appraisals and inspections, and examines report writing with links to parents' evenings.

Appraisal

As an NQT you will be more than aware of the Teachers' Standards (DfE, 2011) and how they have been used to assess your performance. When you come to the end of your first year of full employment the headteacher, informed by your mentor, will decide whether you have met the Standards consistently over a sustained period in your practice and therefore whether you have passed your probationary period. However, the Standards should continue to play an important role in your future career by outlining the practice expected of all qualified teachers. Such an examination of your future performance will form part of the performance management or appraisal arrangements within your school as outlined by the government (DfE, 2012).

Appointment of appraiser

When you have successfully passed your NQT year you may wonder what happens next regarding your appraisal as a teacher. The headteacher will appoint your appraiser from the school staff. In some larger schools they may use a line manager such as a head of department or deputy as your appraiser. However, in smaller settings this could be your headteacher. The appraiser will be tasked with conducting aspects of the annual appraisal cycle, including making pay recommendations if you are eligible. Remember you have the right to object to an appraiser if you feel that you are not going to be judged fairly by the appointed person.

Performance management

Performance management forms what may be seen as a continuous cycle to promote professional improvement. It starts with targets being set through a review and planning meeting. Your performance will then be monitored at specific, identified times throughout the year. Finally, your performance will be reviewed in light of this monitoring to ascertain how successfully you have met the identified targets.

Upon finishing your induction period there will still be aspects of your practice that have been identified as needing to be addressed. These can form the basis of performance objectives for the first year of your performance management.

CASE STUDY

Mitra's experience

I was worried when my mentor mentioned that I would have to have an appraiser next year rather than a mentor. She explained that this would just be part of the school's performance management system and that it would be used to decide whether I would be eligible for an incremental pay rise. I was worried that it would just be someone making judgements about me who did not know me very well or had not really seen me teach. I was worried that they would be visiting me all the time to make observations.

Critical questions

» How can Mitra find out about the performance management in his school?

» Is there a limit to the number of times he will be observed teaching as part of performance management?

» How will Mitra be assessed in the appraisal system?

Mitra should not be worried about performance management since all teachers/school staff are assessed in this way. If he is worried he should talk more to his mentor about this aspect of school life but he should also read the school's performance management policy which will clearly outline the process. Any lesson observations will have been scheduled in advance so he can be well prepared for these events. Generally he would not expect more than one observation per term lasting around an hour. Each observation will have a clearly agreed focus based on the targets set to assess his performance.

The performance management cycle

During your first meeting with your appraiser you should clarify and agree up to three objectives or targets that will provide a focus for the judgement of your annual performance. These targets will be driven in part by your own needs but also by objectives that may relate to the school needs outlined in the School Improvement Plan (SIP). One of your targets should also reflect your professional development aspirations. You will discuss any support you may need to achieve these objectives. The targets set should be precise, measurable, achievable, realistic and linked to a feasible timeframe. Remember any discussion during this meeting should be written up, with both parties keeping copies so that there is never any confusion about what has been agreed before the next part of the cycle begins.

Once your targets have been set, arrangement for monitoring will be put in place and this will involve lesson observations following the school's performance management policy. It will generally involve the appraiser. It may, however, be agreed at the planning meeting that some of the observation will be carried out by another person. Feedback will be given to you on the observations and a copy of the lesson observation form will be shared with you. During this ongoing monitoring stage you will also be kept up to date with your progress through informal discussions.

At the end of the performance management cycle you will have a formal review meeting with your appraiser and this will allow your achievements to be shared and any areas for improvement and professional development to be discussed. After this meeting you will receive a written statement which will outline the agreements from this formal review meeting. It is important that you are happy with this statement since you must agree the final wording of the appraisal statement with the appraiser and add any additional comments you feel are important if they are not covered. If you remain unhappy with any statements remember your school will have an appeals policy. Your performance management discussions and documentation will remain confidential between you and your appraiser, so keep your documents in a safe place. Should things go well your appraiser can make a recommendation that you progress incrementally up the pay progression scale.

Ofsted inspections

Whether you experience an Ofsted inspection in the first year of being an NQT or later in your career will really depend on how long ago your school was last inspected and the last inspection grade it was awarded.

Currently the Ofsted Framework for Inspections (Ofsted, 2015a) allows for 'outstanding' schools to be exempt from routine inspection. However, both Her Majesty's Inspectors (HMIs) who are directly employed by Ofsted and Ofsted itself have the power to inspect a school if its performance deteriorates or should other issues be raised regarding aspects of its schooling, eg child protection issues. Outstanding schools can also be inspected as part of Ofsted's programme of surveys of curriculum subjects or the curriculum in general. If your school is a pupil referral unit, special school or maintained nursery the inspection exemption linked to 'outstanding' status does not apply.

Should your school have been judged to be 'good' then a short inspection will take place approximately every three years. If your school was rated as 'requires improvement' at its last inspection it will be subject to monitoring from inspectors in order to check on its progress and it will normally be inspected within a two-year period from its last inspection. If your school was rated 'inadequate' for aspects of behaviour it could have a no-notice inspection at any time, which means the inspection team will notify your school around 15 minutes prior to their arrival.

The process of inspection

Regardless of whether your school is imminently waiting for an inspection or not, your practice should be continually focused on the *'quality of teaching, learning and assessment, pupils' personal development, behaviour and welfare and the outcomes for children and learners'* (Ofsted, 2015b).

When your school is inspected it will normally be notified around midday on the working day prior to the start of a school inspection. Remember an inspection can happen at any time after five working school days into the autumn term. It is only in exceptional circumstances that an inspection will be cancelled or deferred. Not only will evidence be gathered from what inspectors see in your school but parents will have been notified of the inspection and asked to provide details and views about the provision your school offers.

Inspectors will also look at Parentview to see the views of parents. Parent View may be accessed online and provides parents or guardians of pupils in a school with an opportunity to tell Ofsted their views regarding specific aspects of school life. This includes, for example, the quality of teaching, behaviour and any bullying problems. The survey is always live and therefore individuals do not have to wait until an inspection is called to make comments on this site. Once an Ofsted inspection is called inspectors will visit this site as a means of gaining information and parents' views on a school's performance.

The length of the inspection will not normally be more than two days and the size of the inspection team will be dependent on the size and type of school. The inspection team will usually arrive around 8am on the morning of the inspection and one of the documents required at this early stage of proceedings is a current staff list. The headteacher will be requested to identify you as an NQT on this list so that the inspectors are aware of your new teaching status.

CASE STUDY

Miriam's experience

I was really confused when the headteacher called a meeting of all staff at lunchtime without any real notice. He told us we had just been contacted by Ofsted and that our inspection would commence the next day. He told us to meet firstly as key stage departments and that he would visit each department and then each classroom to check on our progress in preparation for the following day. I was really worried that I would not be ready for the next day and that I would let the team down.

Critical questions

» What important paperwork do you need to have ready before and during an inspection?

» Will the inspectors want to see you teach?

» How will you know how well you and the school are doing?

Though your first thoughts prior to an inspection may be towards trying to attend to matters that concern you and your classroom, such as the quality of the interactive display up on the wall, it is important that you contribute to the team effort needed to prepare for an Ofsted visit. Once you have sorted out any immediate items that may concern you, ask other teachers if they need help in their classroom. Remember that more senior staff may find they are struggling to cover their class-based commitments because of their senior management roles and the additional challenges this brings during an inspection.

The majority of the paperwork you will need for an inspection will have been completed as part of your responsibilities for teaching and learning in your class duties. You will need to make certain it is well organised and easily accessible should an inspector ask to see it.

CHECKLIST

Paperwork

✓   Are your planning and assessment files and records up to date?

✓   Is your SEND file up to date with the relevant documents such as EHCs or provision maps?

✓   Is your NQT file available with evidence that documents your support and mentoring?

✓   Have you any relevant individual lesson plans ready for sessions that an inspector may want to observe?

✓   Is your marking evaluative, consistent and up to date?

✓   Is there evidence that pupils have been set targets?

Observations

Inspectors will spend most of their time gathering first-hand evidence to inform the judgements they are making, including lesson observations. You should be made aware of when you might be observed by an inspector. This could take the form of a joint observation which may involve the headteacher and the inspector who are there to observe and then agree on their graded judgements about the quality of your teaching. You should remember that when an inspector is assessing the strengths and weaknesses of your teaching, learning and assessments they will be taking into consideration where you might be in your development as an NQT rather than as an experienced teacher. Do not be concerned if inspectors talk to pupils during an observation; this is normal practice. They will be using such evidence to assess the quality of teaching and learning as well as evaluating other aspects of personal development.

After the lesson, at an appropriate moment, the inspectors will give you some oral feedback about the quality of what they have observed. This feedback may take a variety of forms, for example, a one-to-one or group discussion of observed teachers. Inspectors will not provide an overall grade for the lesson or for the quality of teaching, learning and assessment. This can be quite disconcerting but what they will have seen in your lesson is only part of the jig-saw of information they will use for making judgements so don't worry if things do not go as well as you would have wished.

Though you will not be present for the final feedback from the inspectors before they leave the school, the leadership team and governors will be told of the grades awarded as a result of the inspection. As soon as is possible this then will be fed back to all staff but these judgements must remain confidential until the report is finally published and therefore made publically available.

Section 48 inspections

If you teach in a school that has a 'religious character' such as a voluntary aided or voluntary controlled school, it will received a Section 48 inspection as well as an Ofsted or Section 5 inspection. The inspectors who will be charged to carry out the Section 48 inspection will be selected by the school's governing body in consultation with the appropriate religious authority such as a diocese. This inspection is not tied to an Ofsted inspection and very much like with Ofsted, the timings are linked to the grading from your school's last inspection. If the grade was good or better an inspection is extremely unlikely to happen again within a five-year period.

The main purpose of a Section 48 inspection is to provide the school and its stakeholders with an evaluation of your school's distinctiveness and effectiveness as a church school. This normally involves one inspector for one day. He or she will ascertain the impact that your status as a church school has on learner achievement and their moral, social and cultural development. With such an inspection RE and collective worship are observed in order for the inspector to gather evidence to inform the judgements made. As with Ofsted should you be observed teaching, which is unlikely given your relative newness to teaching, only general feedback will be offered.

Extra-curricular activities

Extra-curricular activities are an important aspect of school life, and you will be expected to get involved, or even lead, such activities. You should never underestimate the amount of effort that you will invest in this element of school life and how much it will bring to you personally; the school will appreciate it and so too will the parents and more importantly the pupils. It is a chance for you to get to know the pupils outside of class, which can be a real privilege, as well as them getting to see you in a different light.

Before you embark on running any new club you must firstly ascertain if there is a need. You can do this by auditing the current provision and running any idea past your mentor or head-teacher and if necessary contacting the parent body to see if your idea is a goer. You need to consider the following before you start advertising any club to pupils.

CHECKLIST

✓ What age range is best suited to your club?

✓ What sort of pupil will choose your club?

✓ Are there any costs involved in pupils attending?

✓ Does the school have suitable equipment and locations?

✓ How long will each session last?

✓ Is the activity linked to seasonal conditions, eg the weather?

✓ Do you have the prior knowledge and skills necessary to run the club?

Considerations linked to running a club

The school's remission and charging policy will outline if it is suitable for a charge to be levied for such an aspect of schooling. The general guidance will almost certainly state that you can only charge for an activity outside school hours if it is not part of the national curriculum. Also, if more than 50 per cent of the time spent occurs during school hours, it will be deemed to have taken place during school hours and therefore be subject to a voluntary contribution.

Whatever club you decide to run outside school hours you should:

• take a register of attendance so you are aware who has stayed on the premises with you;

• make certain the children are properly supervised at all times and that when you dismiss them they are collected by a responsible adult or parent;

• not allow pupils to be left on their own while they are waiting to be collected;

• make arrangements with other staff who will be responsible for these pupils in your absence if you have to leave early;

• make certain you are aware of where pupils' emergency contacts can be accessed in the school should you need to ring a parent due to an accident or if a pupil remains uncollected.

Residential trips

You may be asked if you would like to attend a residential trip with pupils. This is a wonderful opportunity for you to get to know the pupils over a sustained period and to extend your own professional development. Remember NQTs will not be asked to lead such trips.

CASE STUDY

Sam's experience

I was really surprised when Mr Smith asked me to go with him on the Year 6 trip to York. I was a bit taken aback and did not know quite what to say. He did tell me to think about it so this gave me time to consider this request. I felt worried about whether I would get any sleep, what would happen if a child got hurt or had to be sent home and how much responsibility I would have to take for the trip.

Critical questions

» *Does Sam have to attend the residential trip?*

» *Who will be responsible for organising the trip?*

» *What might Sam need to consider when he is on the trip?*

Sam should only go on the trip if he wants to. He should however not dismiss this opportunity out of hand since it is a wonderful opportunity for him to gain the skills needed in future to run such a trip. He will not be expected to oversee the complete organisation of a residential trip. As an NQT or even RQT this will generally be done by the school's outdoor or educational visits co-ordinator and trip leader, which in this case is Mr Smith. The organiser will:

- organise the transport;
- carry out a pre-visit;
- create or approve the itinerary;
- seek the governors' approval for the trip;
- plan pupil groupings for travel and accommodation;
- be the named responsible adult as an emergency contact;
- complete the associated documentation and risk assessment;
- liaise with parents about the trip.

If you attend a residential visit you must make certain that from the moment that pupils leave the school premises their behaviour is of a high standard, just as you would if they were in school. Though risk assessments for the trip will have been carried out you will still need to be vigilant regarding pupil safety at all times. You should be aware of the itinerary for the trip and any specific needs of the children involved, such as allergies or medical needs. You must also know who the designated first aider is and where you can easily access emergency contact details, medical consent forms and first aid equipment. As with any trip you should at appropriate intervals count pupils/take a role call to make certain all children are accounted for at all times.

If travelling by coach ensure the children are all wearing seatbelts and that they are properly seated while the coach is in motion. Remember the school's child protection policy and procedure must be followed should any associated incident occur. Though pupils may be upset at being away from home, normal protocols should be observed with regard to not putting yourself in any position that could compromise your professional integrity. When you are out of sight of the party leader you should make certain you have their emergency contact details easily available. If a child should find they are separated from your group, make sure they are aware of where to wait and who to talk to. Some schools may issue pupils with a contact card should they get lost or separated; if this is the case make certain pupils have it on them at all times.

Also, all pupils should have vital medication such as inhalers with them at all times. Though such a situation should be avoided, if a pupil needs to use a public toilet a member of staff should firstly check that they are suitable to use and that members of the public are not left unsupervised while your pupils are using the facilities. Finally, if children are using a shop while on their visit, talk to them about getting the right money to hand before going up to the till and checking their change on completion of the transaction. Ask them to check that they can afford all the items they have chosen to avoid unnecessary queues when paying. You should be on hand at the checkout and in the shop to smooth out issues as they arise.

Working with outside agencies

Background overview

You have a duty as an NQT to work with other 'outside agencies' such as health services, police and social care that are sited outside of the immediate school environment. This forms an inter-agency (multi-agency or interdisciplinary) response to safeguarding and the promotion of the well-being of children. Such an approach has its roots firmly embedded in the education system from the gaps found in previous child protection systems. Incidents such as the deeply regrettable death of Victoria Climbie illustrated the need for joined-up thinking and for all agencies involved with children to work together sharing information in order to provide better outcomes for them in the future. The need for such inter-agency working is now enshrined in legislation of which you should be aware. This includes:

- *The Children Act* (DfES, 2004);

- *Every Child Matters* (DCSF, 2003);

- *Safeguarding Children and Safer Recruitment in Education* (DfES, 2006);

- *Safeguarding Disabled Children: Practice Guidance* (DCSF, 2009);

- *Working Together to Safeguard Children* (HM Government, 2015).

The current Special Educational Needs Code of Practice: 0–25 (DfE/DoH, 2015) also clearly signals the need for an integrated approach to the promotion of the well-being and quality of provision for children with special educational needs and disabilities (SEND). Again, through legislation such as the Children and Families Act (DfE, 2014f) and Care Act (DoH, 2014) there should be

> co-operation between children's and adults' services to promote the integration of care and support with health services, so that young adults are not left without care and support as they make the transition from children's to adult social care.
>
> (DoH, 2014, p 38)

Inter-agency working

As a trainee you may have been somewhat shielded from the direct responsibilities associated with working with other agencies. However, as an NQT you will become aware of how an inter-agency approach is vital in securing children's well-being and education. Some issues, such as a pupil's lateness, may lead to a limited need for intervention, while others, such as physical neglect, will prove so complex that there will be a need for an extended collaborative partnership across many agencies. Sometimes the needs of families are so great, such as children in care, that services will be co-ordinated by the local authority. However, this approach may be different given the freedom of academy status since they may wish to co-ordinate the approach taken.

Guidance such as *Working Together to Safeguard Children: A Guide to Interagency Working to Safeguard and Promote the Welfare of Children* (HM Government, 2015, p 13) suggests that professionals like you should, specifically, be alert to the possible need for early help for a child who:

- *is disabled and has specific additional needs;*
- *has special educational needs;*
- *is a young carer;*
- *is showing signs of engaging in anti-social or criminal behaviour;*
- *is in a family circumstance presenting challenges for the child, such as substance abuse, adult mental health problems and domestic violence;*
- *has returned home to their family from care;*
- *is showing early signs of abuse and/or neglect.*

It is the responsibility of the SENCo (Special Educational Needs Co-ordinator) or safeguarding officer to co-ordinate an inter-agency approach, but you may be required to support the assessment process regarding referrals alongside helping to facilitate such an approach in your class-based practice.

There are two main ways in which you might become involved with a child in such an inter-agency approach.

1. Supporting a child on the special educational needs register or who has an education, health and care (EHC) plan or statement.

2. Your role may involve the common assessment framework (CAF) process for those at-risk pupils in your care.

CASE STUDY

Shona's story

I am an NQT. Shona is a 10-year-old pupil who has been in my class for the last term since she arrived from another school. She has been quite aggressive to the other pupils since she arrived and is quick to lose her temper. I know that her mum was not coping since she would often come and find me to tell me how terrible she is at home, that she will not go to bed and that the house is damp and in a poor state of repair. I was really concerned when I looked at her lunchbox and there was just an out of date packet of crisps. I know that Shona is really falling behind with her work and that the old school had her on their SEND register for her behaviour and progress.

Critical questions

» Who should the teacher share her concerns with about Shona?

» What might the teacher have to do as a result of passing on her concerns?

» What range of school-based and other agency support can the school instigate to improve this situation?

Since Shona is on the SEND register the teacher should continue to share her concerns with the SENCo regarding her behaviour and her progress. Much of the teacher's actions will be outlined in Shona's provision map and will involve TA support and perhaps some outside agency help. Both the SENCo and the teacher will need to share their concerns about Shona's home life with the school's safeguarding officer.

It is likely, given the concerns raised, that if not already in place a CAF will need to be set up to co-ordinate and plan a course of support for Shona. This CAF may lead to a 'team around the family' which will involve everyone, including the teacher and parents, being involved in this process. They will share information including observations and assessment records and will make a contribution to Shona's situation as part of a graduated response to meeting her needs.

As a result of such actions the teacher may need to work as part of a team to secure improvements which will help Shona such as improved access to quality food. It may include learning support assistants and publically funded agencies such as behavioural support services or Child and Adolescent Mental Health Services (CAMHS), housing, the school nurse or doctor and a health visitor. Sometimes voluntary agencies may also be accessed in the pursuit of help, such as the National Society for the Prevention of Cruelty to Children (NSPCC).

Though there are obviously many benefits to inter-agency working, since it allows for co-ordinated and timely interventions to issues, you must remember that this approach may sometimes be difficult. Due to patient confidentiality you will not always be able to access information you feel is vital. Also, each agency may have its own agenda which might not always marry with your purely educationally inclusive focus. For example, health care professionals may only be focused on improving health related issues and medical interventions. However, remember that children are at the heart of this process and that you play a vital role in their welfare and happiness.

Working with teaching assistants

Teaching assistants (TAs), learning support assistants (LSAs) or higher level teaching assistants (HLTAs) provide vital support for the children in your care. Depending on your setting, you may have also come across other forms of assistants such as cover supervisors, learning mentors and nursery nurses.

Critical questions

»   *What benefit do support assistants play in your classroom?*

»   *Do you feel you utilise the support to best effect?*

»   *How would you describe your relationship with your TA?*

»   *What role might they take in the learning environment?*

TAs provide an additional pair of skilled hands to support your work with children in class. They can be deployed to generally support children as part of your quality first teaching (QFT). They may also be deployed to support pupils as part of targeted interventions such as Springboard mathematics either on a one-to-one or group basis. Learning mentors may also be deployed by you and used by the school to help pupils with social, emotional and behavioural issues. Though cover supervisors will not be deployed by you they will provide a means for classes to be supervised when staff are absent or on PPA.

CHECKLIST

You might use a TA to:

✓   manage behaviour;

✓   support the delivery of the curriculum;

✓   help with assessments such as observations;

✓   prepare intervention resources.

Effective partnership with your TA

It is important that you remember that not only is a TA paid a relatively small amount of money in comparison to your salary but also that as the class teacher you are the one who is ultimately responsible for the welfare and progress of the children in your class. You should therefore allocate the workload appropriately and help support your colleague in their understanding of effective pedagogy.

One of your greatest challenges as an NQT is establishing a good working relationship with your TA. This can often be hampered by you being new to the setting, or your TA having a pre-formed idea of their role in the class. Sometimes just being much younger than a more established TA who has a wealth of life experience can be daunting. It is therefore important that you establish the ground rules for how you can work together successfully, including clear expectations for your TA and the tasks you would like him/her to undertake.

CASE STUDY

Loren's experience

Loren finds that her TA is always arriving at the beginning of the lesson which provides her with little quality time to talk to the TA about the day ahead and how she will be deployed. Once the TA gets into the classroom she sits down to start listening to what Loren is saying without engaging in any other activity. Later in the lesson, if her TA is not quite certain of the strategies needed when supporting a group, and when a child is misbehaving, she seems to find it difficult to deal with and sends the pupil to Loren.

Critical questions

» *What are the main issues that need resolving between Loren and her TA?*

» *What strategies might Loren put in place?*

One of the major issues in this relationship seems to be communication between Loren and her TA. It would appear that the TA does not really know what is expected of her by Loren once she enters the classroom. It may be that the TA is listening to Loren just to find out what the lesson is about and what she could be doing. It may be that Loren has never really said what she requires the TA to do on her arrival or that they have no means to communicate which tasks the TA should be engaged with on arrival. To address this issue Loren could suggest to the TA that she initiates a communication book which the TA will always find on Loren's desk. Loren could then leave tasks, plans and instructions for the TA to read. The TA could also leave requests or important information for Loren to read. Alternatively, Loren could negotiate with the TA a time outside of teaching, such as before lunch, to share communications. If this is not possible Loren should signal to the TA that she will talk to the leadership team to see if a time can be found to facilitate this. Loren could, if the TA is willing, communicate her wishes by email to the TA the night before class.

Loren also needs to set clear ground rules of what she expects the TA to do if behaviour is an issue, given that consistency is often important for the child. Loren could model strategies she wishes the TA to use and if she has not already done so signal to the child and the TA that the TA's authority is just as valued as Loren's. This can be done by making certain that if the TA wishes to use class-based sanctions to maintain discipline this is fine with Loren and something the child must accept.

As you will come to realise through your NQT year, the TA assigned to you can play a vital part in your success. Alongside all they can bring to the classroom they will also become an invaluable source of information as the year progresses. Since they will know the parents and the year's calendar of events they can help you plan for the expected as well as becoming a sounding board for the unexpected.

Report writing

Though schools have means of communicating with parents such as a home school book or reading diary, legally you must report on a pupil's progress annually. This will include information regarding their engagement with foundation and core subjects, their general progress and achievements (this can include any national test data) and their attendance record. For children with SEND an annual review can form the basis for informing any report writing.

As an NQT you will have never been asked to write an end of year report in full before and for some individuals this can be quite a daunting experience. You will already have a lot of information that can be included in each child's report from assessments already made and the school-based tracking system. You will also know your children well so it is not as overwhelming as it may feel.

Each school will have its own format and timescale for writing reports. The report format and content will also reflect the particular age range of pupils. Reports for children in Reception Year will include details linked to their progress through the EYFS, while at Key Stage 1 they will include general curricular progress as well as outcomes relating to Year 2 SATs results. Reports for Years 3–5 will include general curricular information and assessment information linked to the taking of optional SATs, while Year 6 reports will also include information related to end of Key Stage 2 SATs results.

Some schools use reports to provide summative feedback to parents at the end of the summer term while others use them to provide formative feedback on a child's progress in late spring to promote further pupil progress during the summer term. If the latter is the case, SATs levels are additionally communicated to parents in the summer. Some schools may even use a computer-based system of reporting in order to standardise comments made by staff and to guarantee equity of reporting style.

CHECKLIST

Writing reports

✓   Know your class.

✓   Avoid typographical mistakes.

✓   Keep the report focused.

✓   Avoid copy and paste.

✓   Ask the pupils about hobbies, interests, swimming badges, awards etc.

✓   Use other colleagues' expertise.

To gain an overview of what is required look at previous examples from the school or draft a report and ask a colleague to comment on its style or tone. It is important that the quality of English in reports is beyond reproach, especially given that you may have commented on a pupil's spelling and grammar. Also, given that this document is a means by which you may be informally assessed, typographical errors do not create a good impression regarding the expectations that you set yourself and others. You might find it easier to complete sections such as literacy for a whole class before moving on to another subject, or you could complete each child's report completely and then move on to another child. Remember to find a place and time where you can concentrate and avoid the urge to copy and paste chunks from one report to another. Remember some parents will compare their child's report with that of their friend's child and they wish to see evidence of individuality in the style of a written report. Parents also like honesty and a clearly written report which spells out in plain English what a child has done and needs to do next. Parents should also be left with clear targets that their child needs to achieve to make even greater progress.

Reports have their own particular language, which provides a non-confrontational means of addressing issues which some parents can find upsetting.

Table 4.1 *Reporting phrasebank*

Phrase	Underlying message
Is easily distracted or can distract others	The child is rarely on task and prefers to take up other children's time by talking or causing distractions.
Is careless	The child has ability and the potential to do well but does not focus on making their work accurate. The child has the tendency to make mistakes.
Tries his/her utmost or tries hard	The child is always striving to achieve their best given their ability.
Has yet to learn how to play with others	The child can often fall out with others outside of class and can be unpleasant or cause issues among peers.
Is keen/eager	Is well motivated and eager to engage with learning.
Makes valuable contributions	Is keen and eager to join in with relevant suggestions.
Respects other pupils' opinions	Listens well in class to others' suggestions.
Has a good grasp of...	Is quick to take ideas on board.
Is a respected and valued member of the class	Is trustworthy and liked by the pupils and staff.
Lacks confidence in...	Sometimes find things hard to grasp and can need support.

Table 4.1 (*cont.*)

Phrase	Underlying message
Responds well to small groups or individual support	Sometimes struggles with tasks and needs additional support.
Is a pleasure to teach	Is a lovely pupil.
Needs to consider others' feelings	Can sometimes do and say inappropriate things.

Reports should never contain surprises for parents if you have had effective communication over the course of the year. Be honest, since you will not be thanked if in the following years it looks as if you had not been accurate, but focus on being constructive in your feedback.

Reports are often linked to parents' evenings and schools are required to issue reports well in advance of such a meeting. A lot of parents will bring their report to the meeting so be prepared by having your own copies of pupils' reports to hand and be ready to respond to the comments you have made on them. Make certain you have any relevant assessment data available to corroborate statements made. Remember your headteacher will be on hand if you need assistance and make the headteacher aware in advance if you think you might have a contentious meeting.

Further reading

Bennett, T (2011) *Not Quite a Teacher: Target Practice for Beginning Teachers*. London: Continuum International Publishing Group.

Goepel, J, Childerhouse, H and Sharpe, S (2015) *Inclusive Primary Teaching: A Critical Approach to Equality and Special Educational Needs and Disability*. 2nd ed. Northwich: Critical Publishing Ltd.

5 Past the post

TIMELINE

Past the post

- Strive to be outstanding through the use of the Ofsted outstanding grade descriptors
- Manage your time and workload effectively
- Identify opportunities for professional development activities and promotion
- Complete your induction period

Teachers' Standards

The following Teachers' Standard (DfE, 2011) is applicable to this chapter.

8.   *Fulfil wider professional responsibilities*

   •   *take responsibility for improving teaching through appropriate professional development, responding to advice and feedback from colleagues*

Completing your induction period

Depending on whether you are working full time or part time, or if you have received special dispensation to serve a reduced induction period, you will at some point near the end of induction and move to the next stage of your teaching career. Throughout your final stage of induction you will continue to meet with your induction mentor for professional progress reviews in order to set final objectives, schedule final observations and discuss your final progress report. You will continue to participate in professional development activities, which are discussed in greater detail in this chapter. Finally, you will work with your induction mentor to review your induction period, reflect on the progress you have made, begin outlining objectives and also your CPD plans for your second year of teaching. This will all contribute to the performance management discussions with your reviewer in your second year.

While outstanding teaching is not a prerequisite for promotion, you should be constantly striving to achieve this. CPD is one way in which you can reach your full potential to be an outstanding teacher and subsequently receive promotion. This chapter therefore considers your engagement with CPD and charts how this can positively impact on teaching quality and promotion. Teaching quality is of particular relevance as government reforms have made entry levels into teaching more stringent in order to produce a world-class education system that addresses economic and policy issues to which teachers are held accountable (Dale, 1997).

Outstanding teaching

In order to be judged as an outstanding teacher the full set of standards should be met consistently at a good level or higher. Defining 'outstanding' in the terms of teaching, however, is problematic due to a plethora of reasons. Teaching is not a precise or clear-cut discipline; rather, it is intertwined with complexities and difficulties. Judgements about teaching are further complicated by their subjective nature. With the introduction of one set of Teachers' Standards (DfE, 2011) for unqualified and qualified teachers, the job of identifying best practice has become all the more challenging due to hazy expectations paralleled with the idiosyncratic nature of assessing teachers (Robinson et al, 2015). If as a trainee teacher you were deemed outstanding, you should be aware that the bar rises when you enter your induction period as the expectations placed upon you will increase.

Critical questions

»   *Can you define what outstanding teaching is?*

»   *Where have you witnessed outstanding teaching?*

»   *How did you know it was outstanding teaching?*

»   *What made the teaching outstanding?*

»   *What features were evident?*

»   *What makes an outstanding trainee?*

»   *What makes an outstanding teacher?*

Unpicking what constitutes outstanding teaching is helpful when you are considering how you might continue to develop your practice. It is acknowledged that characteristics of outstanding teaching incorporate high levels of commitment, high levels of confidence, strong levels of subject knowledge and pedagogical knowledge (Grigg, 2010). To be deemed as outstanding you will be expected to take the initiative, be enthusiastic, adaptable and set high expectations. Aspects of your practice may well be regarded as worthy of being shared with a broader professional audience, for example, lesson planning, creative teaching and/or assessment approaches. Inspectors would expect to see *all* pupils in your class making at least the amount of progress you would expect and that this is sustained and consistent over time. It should be noted that Ofsted will not grade any individual lesson that you teach and they observe, as this does not convey the whole picture in relation to teaching, learning and assessment.

The most recent Ofsted (2015a) grade descriptors for outstanding teaching, learning and assessment are given in the table below.

Self-awareness

In order to further enhance your practice you need to know yourself and start to autonomously identify areas for your professional development. This can be achieved relatively simply. For example, you may want to consider videoing yourself teaching and then analyse your performance. This can be (for some) a painful process; however, it could enable you to reap many benefits. It could, for example, help to confirm whether you meet the grade descriptors for outstanding which are defined below. It may also provide you with evidence from your practice that no one previously has shared.

Critical question

»   *Using the table, take a moment to conduct a self-evaluation and identify those areas in which you are striving to be outstanding. Chart your next steps in terms of actions you could take and CPD requirements, and discuss these with your induction mentor the next time you meet.*

Grade descriptor	Next steps/CPD requirements
• Teachers demonstrate deep knowledge and understanding of the subjects they teach. They use questioning highly effectively and demonstrate understanding of the ways pupils think about subject content. They identify pupils' common misconceptions and act to ensure they are corrected.	

Grade descriptor	Next steps/CPD requirements
• Teachers plan lessons very effectively, making maximum use of lesson time and co-ordinating lesson resources well. They manage pupils' behaviour highly effectively with clear rules that are consistently enforced.	
• Teachers provide adequate time for practice to embed the pupils' knowledge, understanding and skills securely. They introduce subject content progressively and constantly demand more of pupils.	
• Teachers identify and support any pupil who is falling behind, and enable almost all to catch up.	
• Teachers check pupils' understanding systematically and effectively in lessons, offering clearly directed and timely support.	
• Teachers provide pupils with incisive feedback, in line with the school's assessment policy, about what pupils can do to improve their knowledge, understanding and skills. The pupils use this feedback effectively.	
• Teachers set challenging homework, in line with the school's policy and as appropriate for the age and stage of pupils, that consolidates learning, deepens understanding and prepares pupils very well for work to come.	
• Teachers embed reading, writing and communication and, where appropriate, mathematics, exceptionally well across the curriculum, equipping all pupils with the necessary skills to make progress. For younger children in particular, phonics teaching is highly effective in enabling them to tackle unfamiliar words.	
• Teachers are determined that pupils achieve well. They encourage pupils to try hard, recognise their efforts and ensure that pupils take pride in all aspects of their work. Teachers have consistently high expectations of all pupils' attitudes to learning.	
• Pupils love the challenge of learning and are resilient to failure. They are curious, interested learners who seek out and use new information to develop, consolidate and deepen their knowledge, understanding and skills. They thrive in lessons and also regularly take up opportunities to learn through extra-curricular activities.	
• Pupils are eager to know how to improve their learning. They capitalise on opportunities to use feedback, written or oral, to improve.	
• Parents are provided with clear and timely information on how well their child is progressing and how well their child is doing in relation to the standards expected. Parents are given guidance about how to support their child to improve.	

Grade descriptor	Next steps/CPD requirements
• Teachers are quick to challenge stereotypes and the use of derogatory language in lessons and around the school. Resources and teaching strategies reflect and value the diversity of pupils' experiences and provide pupils with a comprehensive understanding of people and communities beyond their immediate experience.	

Now consider Kenan's experience and consider the strategies he might adopt in order to improve his practice.

CASE STUDY

Kenan's experience

I knew that I was doing pretty well in my induction period as the feedback I was receiving from my induction mentor was good. My induction mentor was making good suggestions about the things I might like to consider as my next targets and I was in agreement with these. One of the targets set was to observe myself teach, which I found a little odd. How could I possibly observe myself when in full teaching mode? My induction mentor explained that she would like me to video (or audio record) myself teaching the class. I was intrigued as to what benefits this activity would bring to my teaching but went along with it. The thought of watching the recording back was daunting but my induction mentor sat down with me and together we painstakingly reviewed the video frame by frame. It was so illuminating! I was able to identify which aspects of my lesson had gone flat, which pupils were disengaged and subsequently I volunteered my own suggestions as to how I could improve in future. The video also revealed that once I had given a set of instructions to the children, I followed this by asking 'OK?', almost seeking permission from the pupils rather than commanding authority. While it was horrible sitting and watching me teach, it really helped highlight aspects of my teaching that I was not aware of before and that the induction mentor perhaps felt they could not mention. It was a great learning opportunity.

Critical questions

» *What strategies would you use to revitalise a lesson if the pace of learning had slowed?*

» *What do you perceive as the issues around using colloquial terms such as 'OK' and 'like'?*

» *What strategies would you employ to curb the use of colloquialisms?*

» *In what ways do you think video or audio recording could assist in developing your practice?*

Using mini-plenaries to review learning and re-engage pupils is considered good practice and ensures that pace is maintained throughout the lesson. You are encouraged to use mini-plenaries/reviews effectively in the lesson through 'in-practice' reflection (Schon, 1991) or you may have itemised them on your lesson plan. What you want to avoid, however, is a constant interruption of pupils on task; look for appropriate moments when engagement is waning or when you feel that pupils might be struggling to grasp concepts. It is not always easy to be aware of the vocabulary you use in your day-to-day teaching, hence why audio or video recording is beneficial. As the class teacher, you are regarded as a beacon in all that you do and this includes standard spoken and written English. By using colloquialisms, you do not maintain the consistency expected in these areas in order to be deemed outstanding. In addition, the use of 'OK?' after a series on instructions implies that you are seeking permission from the pupils rather than maintaining an assertive and authoritative air in the classroom. Audio and video recording your lessons allows you to check your balance of questioning among the whole class, identify any gender bias or bias towards groups of pupils, and examine and improve how you tackle behaviour issues.

Questioning

To be an excellent teacher, you will need to master the art of effective questioning, which promotes higher-order thinking skills and impacts positively on learning (Cotton, 2001). When teaching, you will need to establish the reasons you are asking the questions in the first place. What are you trying to achieve? Research (Grigg, 2010) demonstrates that teachers often use closed administrative questions rather than open questions, which is what you are striving to achieve. Likewise, teachers often ask questions but fail to give pupils enough time to respond. The best teachers manage to:

* use the full range of questions;

* differentiate the level of questions to suit the abilities of the pupils;

* mentally note the pupil responses;

* assess whether a follow-up question is necessary.

Utilising your TA at this time to record whether pupils have understood is an effective way of deploying additional adults. You will need to balance teacher questions with pupil questions and give pupils time to discuss things in order to explore their thoughts.

Table 5.1 Different types of questions

Type of question	Rationale
Open questions	Used to invite perspectives on topics, to establish new ideas and consider alternatives
Closed (factual) questions	Used to check factual information, accuracy and knowledge
Reflective questions	Used to encourage pupils to think about what might have been done or said in a given context as part of an evaluation or analysis

Table 5.1 (cont.)

Type of question	Rationale
Probing questions	Used to explore themes, problems and characters in order to gain a deeper understanding
Hypothetical questions	Used to pose a theoretical, conjectural situation in the future so that pupils can contribute their own opinions and interpretations
Leading questions	Used to gain acceptance for an explicit interpretation

CASE STUDY

Shona's range of questions

Shona was teaching an English lesson and chose to focus on the story of the *Three Little Pigs*. Within Shona's case study, she asked the pupils the following:

> Well the wolf huffed and puffed until he blew the house down. What do you think of the wolf?... What do you think would stop the wolf?...What would you do if you were one of the pigs?... Destroying the pig's property is wrong, isn't it?... What questions do you have for the wolf?... What happened in the story?

Critical questions

Consider the range of questioning strategies Shona used in the case study. (Note that the duration between questions is not in real time.)

» *Using Table 5.1, can you categorise the types of questions that Shona used?*

» *Which question types did Shona not use?*

» *What questions could you draft for each of these categories?*

» *What characteristics make good questioning?*

The majority of Shona's questions fell into the open question category. She also used a closed question, a leading question and a hypothetical question.

You may want to consider asking your induction mentor or another observer to audit your questioning strategies in a lesson observation. Here are some areas that you may want to focus on.

• Ask your induction mentor to count up how often you question pupils of differing abilities in the course of a lesson. Are you biased towards any of the different ability groups?

• Audit the amount of time you facilitate pupil discussion in lessons. Do you give pupils opportunity to talk to their talk partners?

- Audit lesson plans. Do you write down key questions in advance of lessons? How often are key questions used? How often do you use open/closed questions? How often do your questions fall into the other types of questions?

- Take one of your lessons. How many questions that promote learning did you ask? How many, connected with learning (not procedural, or other), did pupils ask?

- What was the ratio of teacher: pupil questioning? Is this the right balance?

- Classify the types of questions asked in the course of one of your lessons. Analyse the proportions of procedural to educative questions, lower-order to higher-order, open to closed questions etc.

The outcomes from your question audit may inform further CPD opportunities and be included on your NQT professional development action plan.

CHECKLIST

Becoming outstanding

✓ Review your current attainment against the Ofsted grade descriptors and devise a plan of action to help move you to outstanding status.

✓ Organise a date to audio or video record your teaching and review this with your induction mentor.

✓ Make mini-plenaries/review effective learning tools within your lessons.

✓ Get organised and learn how to prioritise.

✓ Strike a work/life balance.

✓ Audit your questioning techniques and strategies.

Time management and organisation

According to Socrates (Patty and Johnson, 1953), working with children could be very stressful. In fact there is a well-known adage advising adults not to work with children and animals! In recent years there has been an increase in the workload, a groundswell of new initiatives, changes to assessment procedures, constant testing of pupils (even among the youngest) and the continuing challenges of managing behaviour within the classroom. There are many points in the school academic year which can be pinch points. How you manage your time and plan for these is essential to your ability to stay on top of things. Take a look at Jamila's scenario below.

CASE STUDY

Jamila's to-do list

I must admit that apart from writing a few reports as a task for my Initial Teacher Training course, I have never written a whole class worth of reports. They are due in a couple of weeks' time and I have barely started them. They are so time-consuming. I just wish someone had told me beforehand so that I could have organised myself a bit more. On top of that I have pupil progress meetings next week and all the assessments to complete. I have marking that is still not finished from a week ago and the display boards need changing. This morning a parent came to see me about their child being bullied. I don't know when I am supposed to sort all these things out. The head also told me that I was to lead an assembly for the whole school on Friday which I am terrified about because I haven't done one before and I just don't know where to start. It will be sports day in two weeks' time and I am theoretically devising some of the team events and organising the prizes. Then there's the everyday planning, teaching and dealing with parents. The head has also asked that we invite our parents in one afternoon before the end of term to watch a lesson of our choosing. That's something else for me to worry about and to organise. I also have to prepare for my meeting with my induction mentor and I haven't had a chance to put any evidence in my NQT portfolio this term. This term's evidence will be used to indicate whether I will pass my induction period. I just don't know where to start.

Critical questions

»   How will you manage report writing?

»   Can any of these duties be delegated?

»   How could Jamila use her time more effectively?

»   Can you establish a priority order for the activities Jamila has outlined that are stacking up on her to-do list and complete the time management matrix below?

Table 5.2 Based on Covey's (2013) Time Management Matrix

	URGENT	NOT URGENT
IMPORTANT		
NOT IMPORTANT		

Having the ability to prioritise is essential, so make yourself a list of the things you have to do and then give them a priority order. Ensure you talk to your induction mentor or another experienced colleague if you are feeling overwhelmed at any point in your induction period. They will be able to reassure you and give you guidance as to what is essential to complete and help schedule your tasks (see Chapter 4 for further guidance).

Professional development

Chapter 1 touched on training courses as a means to further your professional development. In this chapter we examine more closely the range of opportunities available to you in your induction period and beyond. Even as an NQT, you should be thinking about and planning your professional development. Whether you intend to remain a class teacher for the duration of your career or if you are looking to rise up the ranks to senior management in the not too distant future, having well-focused professional development objectives provides a robust sense of purpose and direction to both your short- and long-term aspirations. By prudently considering which objectives you will set for yourself (in consultation with your induction mentor), you will establish a system for reviewing and planning your next steps and any subsequent action. This will enable you to measure your progress against the objectives designated as stepping stones towards your ultimate goal. It also enables you to discuss your progress with your induction mentor at future follow-up meetings and identify any areas that are in need of further enhancement or development. Firstly consider your long-term aspirations. Long-term aspirations are those that are defined as being ten years hence.

Critical questions

»   *What are your long-term aspirations?*

»   *How do you envisage achieving them?*

»   *What are the short- and medium-term goals you need to realise in order to accomplish your long-term aims?*

CPD activities

What CPD opportunities are available to NQTs? Your induction mentor will be best placed to assist you in identifying suitable and appropriate professional development activities. These do not always require attendance at external events and can often be facilitated in-house with other staff with particular expertise.

The following list (while not exhaustive) provides examples of the variety of professional development activities available:

*   curriculum training, for example, English, mathematics etc;

*   NQT induction training;

*   training activities within regular staff meetings and teacher training days;

*   award-bearing courses;

*   best practice research scholarship;

*   other research;

*   visits to other schools/teachers;

*   peer coaching as mentor;

*   peer coaching as mentee;

*   international visit/exchange;

*   exhibitions, conferences, seminars and shows;

* personal reading;

* personal online learning.

Some of the above professional development activities are enlarged upon in the following sections.

Curriculum training

Curriculum training can involve you working with colleages in other schools, perhaps with a focus on moderation or other school-to-school improvement work. It could entail your attendance at a local authority event, or the buying in of a consultant. Often consultants may deliver training at a cluster of schools of which your school is a member. With the demise of local authorities across the country, increased numbers of private providers and universities are offering CPD.

There may be occasions for you to be involved in subject association professional development. For example, if you have a passion for science, technology, engineering or mathematics (STEM subjects) you could get involved in their CPD programme (see Further Reading). Likewise, the National Centre of Excellence in the Teaching of Mathematics (NCETM) provides annual series of professional development training for those working in early years to adult education. Belonging to a subject association can also bring many benefits including access to teaching resources, journal articles and latest research evidence. Joining a subject association often means paying a subscription, so think carefully about which one(s) you would like to be involved with.

NQT induction training

NQT induction training has in the past been facilitated by local authorities. This has been superseded by the involvement of other establishments such as Teaching Schools which are now administrating and supplying NQT conferences. Within your local area, you are advised to ask your induction mentor and/or your appropriate body as to whether there is an NQT/RQT conference available to you. The NQT/RQT conference provides an opportunity to bring teachers at a similar stage of their career together in order to discuss their progress to date. It will consider strategies for developing teaching and learning in your classroom by extending your knowledge of pedagogical practice and embedding your existing practice. Often at these events, leading practitioners and trainers will be invited as keynote speakers in order to inspire your practice going forward into subsequent years of teaching.

Training activities within regular staff meetings and teacher training days

As part of your ongoing development you will have regular weekly staff meetings and teacher training days once a term. Each of these events will entail an element of CPD. Your school will have some key priorities and these will probably feature in the School Development Plan (SDP). Your school may, for example, have a focus on writing or boys' literacy. Whatever the school's focus, you will have dedicated time in staff meetings and teacher training days to work alongside other colleagues in developing the areas of priority. You may also find that governors are invited to attend these events and may ask questions of you and other staff.

Award-bearing courses

There was a drive in the early part of the twenty-first century for the teaching profession to become a Masters profession with the introduction of a national Masters in Teaching and Learning (MTL) qualification. This has since fallen out of favour and funding for the MTL has been withdrawn. There does, however, remain a raft of award-bearing courses that are available to you as an NQT. For example, if you trained to become a teacher at a higher education institution, you may find that you are able to access their Masters level programme at a reduced rate. They are likely to have a specific module for NQTs which would enhance your practice with underpinning theory. Depending on the number of credits you acquire, you may be entitled to a postgraduate certificate, postgraduate diploma or a full Masters award.

Other research

In 2015 the outcomes of the Carter Review were published. Carter called for evidence-based research and practice, in which teachers draw on core skills of how to access, interpret, challenge and use research to inform their classroom practice. There is an increasing expectation that as a classroom practitioner you will be using research evidence to transform teaching and learning in your classroom. You may therefore want to conduct a piece of action research that addresses one of your school's key priorities from the SDP and present your findings at a staff meeting later in the year.

Visits to other schools/teachers

With the advent of school-to-school improvement, professional development is increasingly achievable through visits to other schools and through teachers in your own setting. Leading practitioners have a role in modelling and leading improvement of teaching skills across the sector and as such you can arrange to visit one of them should it be pertinent to your needs.

Peer coaching as a mentor

Believe it or not, as an NQT you will bring certain unique talents and perspectives with you to the school. These may have contributed to the interview panel's decision to appoint you. This means that you may be asked to peer coach a fellow colleague in a particular area. For example, you may hold sporting qualifications in tag rugby while the Year 3 class teacher who happens to teach invasion games has very little knowledge of the area. If presented with the opportunity to peer coach a colleague, see it as flattery, accept graciously, and enjoy sharing the development of effective practice and the ensuing dialogue. Not only will this assist in developing the Year 3 teacher it will also improve your understanding and demonstrate your leadership capabilities and competences. You may be asked to work with this individual over a period of time so ensure you keep records to inform your NQT profile.

Peer coaching as a mentee

A proven professional development strategy is the use of coaching and mentoring for leadership. You should be receiving regular mentoring from your induction mentor. However, there may be others from whom you could benefit in terms of mentoring and coaching. Do not assume that individuals will give their time willingly as teachers are very busy people. However, if between you and your induction mentor you have established that there is a key colleague within the school who could coach you in an aspect of practice, seek them out and ask politely if they would coach you. It may be that you want to take on leadership responsibility on the successful completion of your induction period (see p 85).

International visit/exchange

An international visit or exchange is an excellent way to educate yourself and your pupils. It will also provide you with further enriching opportunities that you will take with you into your future teaching career. For example, Erasmus+ offer staff mobility projects which can include study courses, observations, job shadowing, training and teaching in European countries. These projects invariably last a year; however, individual engagement with the project or travel overseas may take as little as a few days. You may also want to consider taking forward a strategic partnership with a school in order to internationalise your pupils' curriculum. This may be something that you are keen to develop as a RQT, especially if your school does not currently have an international partner.

Exhibitions, conferences, seminars and shows

You may not have considered exhibitions as being a relevant professional development prospect; however, there is a labyrinth of choice available to you. The main event of the academic calendar for many teachers is the Education Show held at the NEC in Birmingham every March. It provides a wealth of free CPD seminars that you can register for. Each seminar lasts approximately half an hour to an hour. In addition to the seminar agenda, you also have chance to mill among the education stands on a voyage of discovery locating new and exciting resources for your teaching. Some schools book a teacher training day so that all the school's teaching staff can attend. There are also subject-specific events throughout the year, often organised by subject associations. You are encouraged to check subject association websites if you are interested in pursuing this in the future; for example, the Association of Mathematics (see Further Reading) holds an annual conference and covers all age ranges.

Personal reading and online learning

In order for you to stay abreast of current developments within education, you should engage in reading around the subject of teaching and learning. Colleagues will often recommend academic texts; however, you are well advised to read the Times Education Supplement (TES) on a regular basis. There are also online learning resources, some of which are free to access. You will need to do your homework in this area however as you are reminded that quality is of the essence.

CPD and the Teachers' Standards

Remember to plan your CPD activities in a strategic fashion rather than ad hoc. Professional development should, ideally, be undertaken with the Teachers' Standards (DfE, 2011) in mind. The examples in Table 5.3 show how you can match an area of the Teachers' Standards that requires development against CPD prospects, next steps and the type of evidence you could you use to substantiate your claim that you can pass the induction period. You could complete a similar table for your own specific needs.

Table 5.3 *Examples of developmental areas mapped to CPD opportunities*

Teachers' Standard	CPD opportunities	Next steps/types of evidence
5. Adapt teaching to respond to the strengths and needs of all students	Attend training on SEN from the local authority's or appropriate body's NQT training programme	Next steps: Look at SEN resources online www.epilepsy.org.uk/info/education www.makaton.org/ www.autismeducationtrust.org.uk/ www.dyspraxiafoundation.org.uk/dyspraxia-children/ www.bdadyslexia.org.uk/information-and-activities/teachers-and-schools.html Try new strategies from SEN course/resources for those with specific needs in the class. Evidence: Lesson plans/resources etc.
8. Fulfil wider professional responsibilities	Observe a governing body or SLT meeting to obtain an understanding of wider school leadership	Next steps: Contribute to the whole school and attend other relevant training in order to understand leadership across the school. Evidence: Keep a log of professional development that demonstrates how the observations have improved your own practice.

CHECKLIST

CPD

✓ Consider your short, medium- and long-term aspirations and plan accordingly.

✓ Identify which Teachers' Standards you need to work on and organise appropriate CPD opportunities to address these needs.

Progression and promotion

As you draw to the close of your induction period your mind may wander to the prospect of promotion, the possibility of an increase in salary and the next steps towards achieving your medium- and long-term goals. Hopefully, one of your short-term goals will have been realised with the successful completion of your induction period. But what might your career trajectory look like moving into the near future and what steps should you take next?

Use of social media

Believe it or not, social media is playing an increasingly large role in recruitment, progression and promotion. Headhunters frequently use social media, in particular professional sites such as LinkedIn, to scan your curriculum vitae and then offer you opportunities that you may not otherwise have heard about. You may be very happy at the school in which you completed your induction period. However, you may want to consider setting up a LinkedIn page for professional contacts and opportunities.

Becoming a subject co-ordinator

With the successful completion of your NQT induction period under your belt, it is highly likely that you will be approached by the headteacher (or one of their senior leadership team) to enquire as to what area of the curriculum you would like to lead. You cannot always choose; for example, English and mathematics co-ordination usually falls to someone with greater experience in the first instance due to the significant part these subjects play in pupils' learning and in Ofsted inspections. The role of subject co-ordinator may not be remunerated in the first instance but it is a logical step in terms of your career progression. Consider what knowledge, support and skills you may require as a subject co-ordinator.

Critical questions

» *What knowledge will you need of the subject?*

» *What knowledge will you need of practice?*

» *What knowledge will you need of resources*

» *What knowledge will you need of attainment?*

» *Who will you support?*

» *Where and who will support you?*

» *How will you monitor attainment?*

» *What will you monitor on lesson plans?*

» *How will you monitor pupils' work?*

» *How will you monitor teaching?*

» *How will you plan to develop your subject?*

» *What items do you believe should appear in a subject co-ordinator's file?*

In the first instance you will need to have a good knowledge and understanding of the theory underpinning your chosen subject, appreciate the teaching methods and programmes of study and the other expectations, including those of Ofsted. In terms of practice, you will be familiar with pedagogical approaches and practice across the school. If you are not aware of the practice across the school, then you will need to arrange to meet with colleagues in order to discuss this. You will probably need to complete an audit and gap analysis of the resources for your subject across the school. Use your time at one of the CPD events to ascertain what new resources might be available and find out how to order them. Remember however to check with your headteacher what size of budget your subject has allocated to it and stay within it. You should know how well pupils attain in your subject and if this is in line with expectations.

You will be expected to support colleagues with planning, and define a curriculum policy with a scheme of work. You should be able to demonstrate good practice when supporting teaching, working alongside colleagues and providing advice. You may need to provide information and present opportunities to governors, non-teaching staff, parents and children so that they can get involved with the subject at points throughout the year if they desire.

You should be able to monitor trends over time in attainment. Year on year you should make comparisons, identify if there are any groups who exceed expectations or those groups that fall below the benchmark. Another monitoring role you will be expected to undertake is that of planning. As a subject co-ordinator you will need to compare lesson planning from each year to ensure that there is progression across a scheme of work, that learning objectives are clear and that teachers are differentiating. You will need to monitor children's work in association with lesson planning to see that the two align and scrutinise teacher feedback and marking to ensure that pupils are set appropriate targets and are achieving. Finally, you will observe and monitor teaching, providing teachers with feedback and report findings at staff meetings.

In developing your subject area you will be expected to build on existing good practice and identify and improve any areas of weakness.

The following items might appear in a subject co-ordinator's file:

- a copy of the current subject policy;

- the relevant 'subject' part of the School Development Plan as appropriate;

- Ofsted comments from the last inspection associated with the subject;

- an audit of curriculum management, to include a copy of the co-ordinator's action/ development plan, a list of jobs to do and when etc;

- resources;

- a copy of the scheme of work along with a curriculum map showing when the units will be delivered in the year;

- a copy of teacher's planning;

- monitoring schedule and monitoring reports;

- any assessment information that is useful, eg SATs results and analysis, other test results, teacher assessments;

- a record of the budget set and expenditure against this.

6 Ongoing considerations

Be prepared for the unexpected...

TIMELINE

Ongoing considerations

- Look after yourself and safeguard others
- Expect the unexpected and manage unplanned events
- The Prevent Strategy and other issues of professionalism

Teachers' Standards

The Teachers' Standards (DfE, 2011) consist of two parts: Part One outlines the expected standards for teaching, and Part Two sets out the personal and professional expectations of teachers in England. The wider responsibilities of a teacher are included in the Teachers' Standards because the professional role extends beyond the classroom, so attention to

Teachers' Standard 8 is vital (see below). Although Part Two is primarily used to make judgements regarding misconduct, it would be useful to make yourself aware of these standards, particularly in relation to your response and behaviour during unplanned or unexpected events linked to your teaching career.

8. *Fulfil wider professional responsibilities*

- *make a positive contribution to the wider life and ethos of the school*

- *develop effective professional relationships with colleagues, knowing how and when to draw on advice and specialist support*

- *deploy support staff effectively*

- *take responsibility for improving teaching through appropriate professional development, responding to advice and feedback from colleagues*

- *communicate effectively with parents with regard to pupils' achievements and well-being*

Part two of the Teachers' Standards: personal and professional conduct

A teacher is expected to demonstrate consistently high standards of personal and professional conduct. The following statements (DfE, 2011) define the behaviour and attitudes which set the required standard for conduct throughout a teacher's career.

- *Teachers uphold public trust in the profession and maintain high standards of ethics and behaviour, within and outside school, by:*

  - *treating pupils with dignity, building relationships rooted in mutual respect, and at all times observing proper boundaries appropriate to a teacher's professional position*

  - *having regard for the need to safeguard pupils' well-being, in accordance with statutory provisions*

  - *showing tolerance of and respect for the rights of others*

  - *not undermining fundamental British values, including democracy, the rule of law, individual liberty and mutual respect, and tolerance of those with different faiths and beliefs*

  - *ensuring that personal beliefs are not expressed in ways which exploit pupils' vulnerability or might lead them to break the law*

- *Teachers must have proper and professional regard for the ethos, policies and practices of the school in which they teach, and maintain high standards in their own attendance and punctuality.*

- *Teachers must have an understanding of, and always act within, the statutory frameworks which set out their professional duties and responsibilities.*

Beyond the classroom: anything can happen

As a teacher most of your focus will be on your pupils: their needs, their progress and their attainment. You will also be aware of the wider life of the school, and the community of which you are now a part. However, it is important to realise that events cannot always be predicted. Things will happen during your career, and possibly during your NQT year, in the most unexpected ways, both good and bad. This chapter deals with some of the sudden events that might affect you.

It is also important to consider aspects of professionalism and conduct that can and should be anticipated but are often overlooked until a problem arises, by which time it may be too late for a positive outcome. The same can be said about issues of health and well-being. It is important that you are aware of your own and others' responsibilities to ensure your NQT year (and future career) go as successfully as possible.

Health and well-being: looking after yourself and others

The *School Teachers' Pay and Conditions Document 2015 and Guidance on School Teachers' Pay and Conditions* (DfE, 2015d, pp 47–8) states that:

> A headteacher may be required to undertake the following duties: Promote the safety and well-being of pupils and staff; [...] Lead and manage the staff with a proper regard for their well-being and legitimate expectations, including the expectation of a healthy balance between work and other commitments.

This is a clear statement about your employer's duty to consider your health and well-being, but it does not mean you do not take responsibility for looking after yourself. Teaching is a physically and mentally demanding job, and you need to make sure you are paying attention to your own health in order to be effective in the classroom.

Critical questions

» *Before you became a teacher what hobbies and interests did you have? Have you managed to maintain any or all of these around your school responsibilities?*

» *What sort of "brain break" do you use to ensure you are energised and refreshed:*

- during the working day/term?

- during school breaks?

While physical health issues can mean you are unable to keep going without seeking help, your mental health can be under considerable pressure for some time before you realise you need to look after it. By maintaining a hobby or interest, and by building in timely breaks from your normal working patterns, you will be able to establish a better work–life balance. If these things begin to be difficult to maintain this is a good indicator of the need for a conversation with your mentor or headteacher about how they can support you.

The NHS Choices website (www.nhs.uk/Conditions/stress-anxiety-depression/Pages/mindfulness.aspx) suggests five simple steps you can take to improve your mental health (see Figure 6.1). It is worth considering if any are missing from your current lifestyle:

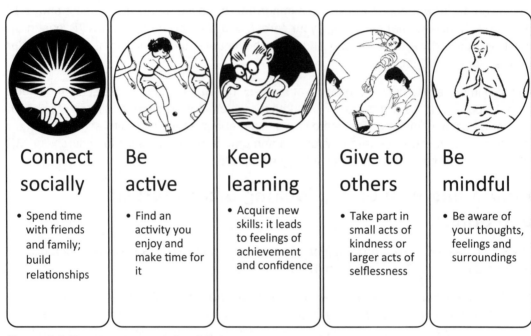

Figure 6.1 *Five steps to mental well-being*

Discrimination and protected characteristics

Sometimes mental well-being suffers due to discrimination and it is worth being aware of what counts as a protected characteristic according to the Equalities Act 2010. It is an offence to discriminate against a person based on their:

- *age;*
- *being or becoming a transsexual person;*
- *being married or in a civil partnership;*
- *being pregnant or having a child;*
- *disability;*
- *race including colour, nationality, ethnic or national origin;*
- *religion, belief or lack of religion/belief;*
- *sex;*
- *sexual orientation.*

(HM Government, no date)

However, although the Act means you are legally protected at work, a situation may arise that makes you feel uncomfortable.

CASE STUDY

Gary's experience

During my final school experience while I was a trainee something happened that made me wonder if I even wanted to be a primary teacher. I had been at the school for three weeks. Every Monday morning the head led a staff briefing where the week's events were discussed and the calendar was shared. On this Monday, my fourth in the school, the head stood up and said, "I have an email here that says a tutor wants to visit someone called Gary. Does anyone know who Gary is?"

This might not have seemed so bad if it wasn't for the fact that I was the only male in the school; also, there was only one class in each year group, so my presence in the school should not have been a surprise to the head!

After this it seemed as if I couldn't do anything right. The head would suddenly appear during my lessons, walk around the classroom without acknowledging me and then leave, only to send a message via my mentor about keeping my marking up to date or tidying up my classroom. My lesson observations were all good, but these were all with my mentor and she didn't seem to have a problem with my teaching or classroom management.

I secured my first teaching post and in my first review meeting I discovered that the previous headteacher had written a really poor reference which didn't reflect my time in her school at all.

Critical questions

» Was Gary the victim of discrimination?

» If this sort of situation arose in the workplace what support is available?

CASE STUDY

Kath's experience

I had spent many of my teenage years hiding the fact that I am gay. My family and community are particularly religious and I didn't think they would understand. While I was at university I began to feel more confident about who I was; changes to legislation, for example, the change to marriage laws that meant one day I might be able to get married to my partner, made me feel like the world was becoming a more accepting place.

When I started my new job as an NQT I didn't feel the need to announce my sexual orientation, and on the second day I was relieved: during a discussion about teaching relationships another staff member asked the head if we should be discussing same-sex families with the children. Her reply was an absolute no; when pushed she said that we didn't have that sort of thing in our area so it wasn't relevant. Later she was overheard saying that it would be a real problem to have same-sex parents, or even worse, gay staff, at the school.

Critical questions

»   *Is Kath the victim of discrimination?*

»   *How should she handle the situation?*

Both Gary and Kath were made to feel uncomfortable in a work environment, and both situations involve protected characteristics (gender and sexual orientation). In Gary's case it is unclear if the headteacher was discriminating against him because he is male; had he stayed in the school he may have felt it was more a case of workplace bullying than discrimination. In Kath's case, however, there is clearly an issue for the headteacher regarding sexual orientation and Kath may wish to seek advice from her union regarding her rights in the workplace. The University of Worcester has a section on their website called *Creating Positive Classroom Cultures* and this includes links, guidance and advice about tackling issues of homophobic, biphobic and transphobic bullying for staff, pupils and families. It can be found at www.worcester.ac.uk/discover/education-creating-positive-classroom-cultures. html. Your training institution may have a similar site.

Safeguarding

Chapter 4 included some issues around safeguarding, particularly with regard to children with SEND or other specific concerns. However, as a classroom teacher you have a duty of care towards all your pupils, particularly in terms of community cohesion, as part of the Education Act 2002 requirement to promote pupils' spiritual, moral, social and cultural (SMSC) development. This requirement has been clarified and developed in light of the *Prevent Strategy* (HM Government, 2011), which was developed to tackle the radicalisation of young people in order to prevent them becoming involved in extreme terrorist activities.

British values, radicalisation and the Prevent duty

> *From 1 July 2015 all schools, providers and registered later years childcare providers (referred to in this advice as 'childcare providers') are registered early years childcare subject to a duty under section 26 of the Counter-Terrorism and Security Act 2015.*
>
> (DfE, 2015c)

The Teachers' Standards Part Two (DfE, 2011) provide a clear expectation that teaching staff in schools will not undermine the values deemed to be mainstream in British life in the *Prevent Strategy* (see Further Reading section for access details). These values specifically include:

•   democracy;

•   the rule of law;

- individual liberty;
- mutual respect;
- tolerance of those with different faiths and beliefs.

In November 2014 the DfE provided further departmental advice for maintained schools around how to actively promote British values as part of the SMSC curriculum; the document, *Promoting Fundamental British Values as Part of SMSC in Schools*, also detailed Ofsted's specific focus on SMSC during Section 5 inspections. There is similar guidance for independent schools within the *Independent School Standards* (ISS). While some of these documents offer non-statutory guidance, many schools have chosen to follow the suggested course of action on the understanding that Ofsted will be looking for evidence to support the promotion of British values rather than simply evidence that staff are not undermining them, (as indicated in the Teachers' Standards (DfE, 2011). There are many resources and materials being developed to support the development of values within SMSC, but it would be useful to read the DfE and government publications. These are regularly updated and always indicate review dates to help you stay abreast of developments.

CASE STUDY

Nikodem's story

I work in an urban school within a diverse community. The school liaises really well with local community and faith groups, and there is a big focus on community cohesion.

We started to notice that many of our older Muslim pupils, particularly the Year 6 boys, were distancing themselves from the rest of the school. In lessons they began to refuse to do what the female TAs said, and were increasingly reluctant to take part in class discussions or activities. Then the younger sister of one of the boys told her teacher she was really worried because she had overheard her brother tell his friends that non-Muslim people at the school didn't deserve to live.

Critical questions

»   *In light of the Prevent duty (DfE, 2015c), what course of action does the school have to take?*

»   *Should the family/local community be involved? If so, how might this be accomplished in a way that promotes community cohesion?*

»   *Would the issue be the same if the pupils involved were*

-   younger?

-   older?

-   not pupils but staff members?

There is no expectation that an individual teacher will take sole responsibility for tackling issues such as these as it is a whole school obligation. However, if you are in any doubt as to how to respond then referring to the statutory duties and non-statutory guidance found within the documents mentioned above will help. There are also Workshop to Raise Awareness of Prevent (WRAP) training courses, accredited by the Home Office, available to support all staff.

Cyber safety and digital worlds

As part of the *Prevent* duty (DfE, 2015c) schools are reminded of the need to protect children from extremist materials and terrorist activity when online. Using appropriate security settings and filtering internet access in school will help, and it is worth talking to the person responsible for this in your setting to discover what is considered appropriate. In one school, pupils searching for Arsenal Football Club found themselves getting warnings that they were attempting to access inappropriate content by using offensive language (it is difficult to spell Arsenal without the offending term!).

However, children are often able to access the internet using unfiltered routes, particularly now that mobile phone and digital technology has meant most technological devices have some sort of embedded connectivity. With this in mind it is more important than ever that you are fully aware of how to maintain privacy, stay safe and avoid harm online, and that you are able to help children manage the risks. It is also worth remembering that you have a statutory duty to '*maintain high standards of ethics and behaviour, within and outside school*' as part of the Teachers' Standards (DfE, 2011), and this includes your online behaviour.

CHECKLIST

E-safety

✓   Read the school's e-safety policy.

✓   Identify ways to report inappropriate behaviour online, including the Report Abuse button and individual website protocols.

✓   Maintain an awareness of new and popular social media (this will help you make judgements about suitability if you learn of pupil use).

✓   Use the CEOP and Thinkuknow websites to teach children about internet safety.

✓   Run awareness raising events for parents and encourage them to discuss their own online safety measures with their children. For example, you could explain how to set a secure password, the importance of privacy settings, etc.

✓   Pay attention: children may not understand the significance of some of the events happening online, which makes them vulnerable to grooming and other forms of exploitation, so be aware of key indicators.

There are several websites in the Further Reading section that will help you develop your own understanding of cyber safety.

Managing planned and unplanned events

You can sometimes find yourself managing visitors to your classroom who want to know exactly what is going on. Teachers can expect to experience visits from Her Majesty's Inspectorate (HMIs) for Ofsted inspections (see Chapter 4) and monitoring visits (where appropriate), governors and School Improvement Advisers (among others) and while this should not be a torturous process, it can feel daunting. In some cases a little preparation and forethought will be enough to make the visit pass smoothly; in other cases more extensive planning is required.

Open evenings and school fairs

Open evenings often happen in the autumn term to enable parents and carers to make decisions about where to apply for their children's school places. Families can choose up to three prospective schools and rank them according to preference. If your school is oversubscribed or in a healthy catchment area with a generally high intake of pupils each year you may feel the open evening is a formality, but it is important that you understand the significance of the event for the families that attend: for most they are making important decisions that will affect the next seven years of their children's lives.

School fairs are usually fundraising events that help the school buy resources or take part in wider opportunities, but they are still occasions where parents get to experience the values and ethos of the school. For this reason they should be treated similarly to open evenings.

The whole school is likely to have a 'tidy up' ready for the open evening, but there are reasons for this beyond the cosmetic. Schools have expensive equipment and hold a lot of sensitive data about pupils, some of whom could be particularly vulnerable. It is vital that you pay attention to how you store records and documents about pupil progress or personal circumstances. Records should be removed or stored securely in the classroom, and children's belongings should be in storage trays or sent home. The classroom environment should be tidy, but it should also be secure, with no valuables left where they can be easily accessed.

If pupils are to be involved in the open evening, discuss how members of the public should be greeted, even if they are familiar to the children – other prospective parents may not be aware of the relationship and will make judgements about the school based on how they see the pupils interact with the visitors. Every member of staff and every pupil is an ambassador for the school, and they should all be clear as to their role.

Open evenings should be enjoyable, but there are matters that can arise that can cause disruption if not handled appropriately. Local feuds, parental disputes or perceived issues with an aspect of the school can sometimes lead people to disregard the fact that they are at a family event, so it is worth discussing with your mentor what the procedure is should an issue arise, particularly if staff members are spread throughout the school. More serious issues, such as banned persons attempting to access the premises, should also be discussed and clear strategies outlined, as the very openness of the event may make the usual security procedures difficult to follow.

CHECKLIST

Open evening

✓ Ensure all confidential documentation is appropriately stored and concealed.

✓ Remove valuables and personal belongings, or secure them in a suitable location.

✓ Sort through classroom resources and remove or discard broken or damaged items.

✓ Ensure all displays are complete and in a good state of repair.

✓ Replace displays that are tatty or dated.

✓ If pupils are involved in the event, set ground rules and expectations for behaviour, uniform (if appropriate).

✓ Remember to check if there are any safeguarding issues to be aware of, eg particular individuals who are not allowed on the premises.

Professional visits

In addition to Ofsted and HMI, there are several different visitors who may come to the school in order to look at practice and pupil attainment. School Improvement Advisers from a School Improvement Partner (SIP) will be involved with a school in order to help and advise as critical professional friends, as opposed to passing judgement. It is their role to help a school evaluate its performance, identify key priorities and plan effective change. As a result they may visit your classroom to observe and offer guidance; visits should be planned in advance and you should have a clear understanding of the purpose of the visit. If in doubt, ask: it is important that you are aware of exactly what they have come to help you with, and this will also help you ensure you have everything to hand that may be needed to make the visit productive.

Governors who have responsibility for a particular subject area or other aspect of school management may want to come and see the school during the working day to develop their understanding of how the curriculum is taught or behaviour managed. Local headteacher networks sometimes arrange Learning Walks in different schools to share good practice and offer advice in addressing areas in need of improvement. Again, these should be planned in advance and there should be a set procedure for how a Learning Walk is conducted. Some unions have provided draft Learning Walk model policies which indicate what is acceptable under the terms and conditions of your employment, and it is worth investigating these if there is not an existing policy in your setting.

Local dignitaries, guest speakers and royal visits

Having settled into your role, you may feel ready to arrange a visit from an outside speaker. The school may have a set protocol and draft letter for such an invitation, so do check whether this is available. If you are drafting your own letter or email then it is worth checking what the headteacher's preference is regarding the use of the school logo or letterhead; also check whether the head needs to see any communication before it goes out into the public domain.

The internet is often a great source of information regarding how to contact different individuals. Publishers or agents often manage the events diaries of children's authors; town clerks may be the best place to start if you wish to invite the Mayor or local council members into school. Prior to sending the invitation, however, make sure you investigate associated costs and who will cover them as the school may not be able to afford unexpected travel and accommodation costs on top of a speaker's fee. Once an invitation has been sent and accepted ensure you communicate with the appropriate person to clarify expectations about the day on both sides. You will need to discuss with them what sort of space is required, whether there is a maximum number of participants that can be involved, whether any particular resources are needed, what the intended content of the speaker's presentation is, etc. This will help the event go smoothly.

A more unusual type of visit may be one from your local MP, a government minister or even a member of the Royal Family. The protocols and procedures around these visits are dictated by the appropriate office; for example, in the case of the Royal Family it is the local Lord-Lieutenant. In each county there will be a Lord Lieutenancy (details can be found at www .royal.gov.uk/TheRoyalHousehold/OfficialRoyalposts/LordLieutenants/LordLieutenants. aspx) who will be able to advise you on sending an invitation. As schedules are worked out well in advance it is advised that you send an invitation at least six months prior to the suggested visit, so if you wanted a member of the Royal Family to open the school's newest building you need to plan for this well ahead.

Once an invitation to an MP or member of the Royal Family is accepted you will be fully informed as to what to expect, particularly with regard to security, policing and the details of the visit. One key thing to consider is that the details of the visit must be kept confidential for security reasons and that details must only be released through official channels.

National and international tragedies and disasters

Sometimes unexpected and unforeseen situations arise that need careful management and sensitivity, both for yourself and for others. This can be as the result of an accident or tragedy that affects you and the pupils directly or indirectly. In 1997 staff in schools found themselves having to help children deal with an outpouring of public grief at the death of Princess Diana; in 2001, when a terrorist attack brought down the Twin Towers in New York, the constant media coverage and sense of public shock also entered the classroom. The same happened again during the 2015 Paris terrorist attacks. In situations like these it is important to remember that you have a personal and professional role to play in supporting your pupils.

The increased use of social media and the 24/7 nature of news coverage means that global events can affect children more quickly and vividly than ever before. They often witness scenes of terrorism, violence and tragedy simply while walking past a newsstand during a family shopping trip, or by listening to the news on a car radio. Ignoring these events may leave children feeling confused about the circumstances or even traumatised with no way of expressing how they feel.

Whenever a tragedy or natural disaster occurs the staff in school should agree a course of action. If this is not forthcoming, it is worth discussing with your mentor how to approach the topic.

CASE STUDY

Naomi's story

I was an NQT in 2004, when Thailand and other countries in the Indian Ocean were swamped by a tsunami. Even though it happened on Boxing Day while the children were on holiday it was all my Year 3 class wanted to talk about when they returned to school in the New Year. By break time we realised as a school that all the children were concerned about what had happened, especially as we live in a river town that regularly floods: some of the younger children were frightened that a tsunami might come up the river!

The headteacher decided to hold a special assembly after lunch. She talked about what happened and showed the children a map up on the projector screen to show them where Thailand was in relation to the UK. She talked briefly about the kind of flooding we experience in our local area and how it was different to a tsunami. She then asked all of the children to go back and have circle time (a strategy which was not commonly used in our school) with their class teachers to talk about what had happened and to make suggestions of ways we could help.

I was really pleased the head had taken the issue seriously as a whole school one, but suddenly I found myself having to do a circle time for the first time about a very serious and emotive issue. I didn't know where to start, and I was really nervous about making the children more upset than they already were.

Critical questions

»   How would you facilitate such a discussion?

»   How can you ensure pupils feel emotionally and physically safe both during and after the discussion?

Use the planning aid in Figure 6.2 to think through ways you could organise a discussion around sensitive issues.

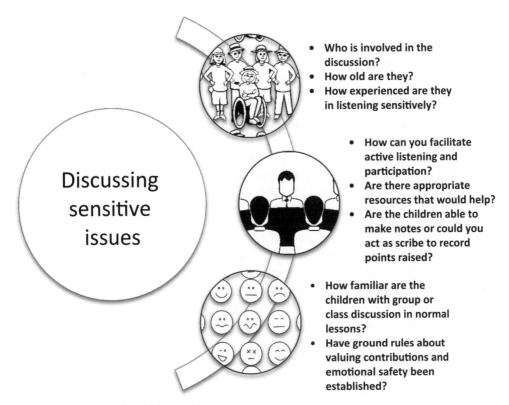

Figure 6.2 *Planning tool to aid sensitive discussions*

Key to any discussion is a confident understanding of how to use spoken language. It is important that you develop this as part of the pupils' everyday curriculum and then, should the need arise, they will be able to handle mature and meaningful discussions around more difficult topics. Mercer (2000) provides a useful theoretical explanation of how to establish effective talk in the classroom which will help underpin your practice.

Professional tragedies and disasters

Sometimes a natural disaster, accident or tragedy will happen much closer to home, and while many of the issues discussed in the previous section may still be relevant there is the added emotional distress that comes with knowing the people involved. This affects both staff and pupils. These are examples of some of the unplanned life events that have actually happened to trainees, NQTs, teachers and pupils within the last 10 years:

- sudden death of the class teacher and trainee mentor;

- suicide of the headteacher on school premises;

- coach accident during a school skiing trip resulting in the death of a staff member and injury to several pupils;

- suicide of a Trans teacher (after significant media interest in her transition);
- stabbings involving the death of staff members and pupils, both on school premises and out of school premises.

These events are not common, but they do happen. You should be offered support and counselling by your employer, and if you are a member of a union they will also have support mechanisms in place to help you through a difficult time. The Board of Governors, academy trust and/or any other relevant body involved in the running of the school should keep you fully informed of the policies and procedures they wish you to follow, but ensure you know to whom you can and should address questions, especially in the event that the headteacher is not available to answer them.

Dealing with the media

When a tragedy or disaster happens there is likely to be media interest. If you work in a maintained school then the local authority should have a communications and press office; if you are part of an academy trust it is likely they will also have a central office which will take responsibility for communicating with members of the media. It is worth making yourself aware of the procedure for dealing with media communication within your organisation, as you could inadvertently put yourself and others in a vulnerable position, legally and morally, if you provide information which becomes part of the public domain. Again it is worth remembering that Part Two of the Teachers' Standards requires you to *'maintain high standards of ethics and behaviour, within and outside school'* (DfE, 2011): this includes your behaviour on social networking sites as well as in person. A comment to a journalist or online, no matter how secure you thought it was, can be shared by others and thus taken out of your control.

Critical questions

» *What is your school's policy for dealing with the media in the event of a tragedy or natural disaster?*

» *How can this be shared effectively with staff?*

» *Who is directly affected by the policy? Who is indirectly affected?*

Think about how this information has been communicated to you, and if it hasn't then think about who you may need to raise this with. It is also worth considering how those indirectly affected might need to be treated when the procedures are in place: how much information can you share with other staff, parents and pupils, for example? It is not unreasonable to ask for guidance on an agreed wording for responding to queries from the press or members of the public.

Personal events

Sometimes events can happen in your personal life that affect your ability to concentrate on your role.

CASE STUDY

Katie's experience

During my NQT year my mother was diagnosed with cancer. It was aggressive and she needed extensive surgery and treatment. I didn't live with my parents but I was close enough to visit regularly and at times I felt I should be with my mother rather than at work. I didn't really know what I could do: was I allowed to take compassionate leave to support a parent?

Critical questions

» *Who do you think Katie should have talked to about her situation? Do you think anyone at work needed to know?*

» *How can you find out what your rights as an employee are before something happens?*

Your contract should outline the conditions of employment, including your rights, as well as your duties, so it is worth having a look at the terms and conditions you signed regarding your employment and discussing things with your headteacher.

CASE STUDY

Katie's experience continued

Then, in May, my mother passed away. Even though we knew she was very ill it was still unexpected: she deteriorated quickly and died within a week of being admitted to hospital. I didn't know what to do about work: I was dealing with my grief, helping my dad cope and also trying to arrange a funeral, but (silly as it sounds) I was also worried about not being in the classroom and finishing my NQT year. I didn't know if taking time off would affect my job in a negative way, which made me feel I had to rush back to work.

As mentioned in Chapter 1, union membership can be very helpful. In situations like that faced by Katie, when you are dealing with intense emotional stress, it can be difficult to think about the practicalities of your rights and responsibilities. Union membership often offers legal guidance and support; and they will know the appropriate legislation that applies in your case. They should also be able to answer questions about the implications for you in the workplace. What they can also offer in most cases is guidance and support for your own health and well-being.

When parents separate

It is not just you as a teacher who may be facing difficult personal circumstances: your pupils may also have issues at home that are affecting them and their ability to concentrate. While many people find it easy to be compassionate about a family bereavement or personal injury there is less support offered when the personal issues centre around separation and divorce.

CASE STUDY

A mother's experience

While my children were of primary school age my marriage ended suddenly. I hadn't realised anything was wrong until, in the first week of the autumn term, the children's father left saying he didn't want to be married anymore. I was devastated, and so were the children. Their father moved out of the family home at the weekend and now lived over an hour away, meaning I was solely responsible for school pick-ups and drop-offs.

I went in to see the class teacher to explain what had happened. She was sympathetic at first, but when I became overcome by emotion about how this might affect the children in the long term she said, "Don't worry, they've just joined the 60 per cent of children from broken homes".

I couldn't believe it. Not only was the phrase "broken home" highly upsetting, the idea that my children were going through something she saw as fairly common just made me wonder how well the school was really doing when it came to the pupils' emotional well-being. I'm sure she thought she was being comforting, but in reality it made me feel that the school could not help me to support my children.

Critical questions

>   How do you think the class teacher should have handled the conversation?

>   What is the class teacher's responsibility in this situation, in both the short and long term?

>   What support is available for families going through separation and divorce?

Unless you have personal experience of separation and divorce you may not understand all the implications. Even if you have experienced it, either as a child or as an adult, your experience may be very different to that of your pupil's family. If the situation has arisen because of domestic abuse or violence then there may be a number of agencies involved, for example, the police and family courts or social care services. However, in many cases the parents are alone in trying to sort out the details of their new family circumstances.

CASE STUDY

A father's experience

My daughter was only a toddler when her mother and I split up. When she started Reception the school were really good: they sent us both copies of her reports and any newsletters, and they used my email address to keep me updated about parents' evenings etc. I worked away *and wasn't able to help regularly with childcare, so without their efforts I would have found it difficult to keep up with what was happening.*

Then, when her mother was in a new relationship, they moved house and my daughter had to start a new school. This time the headteacher was adamant that only one set of reports and documents would be sent out; it was a church school, and they implied that they didn't agree with divorce and therefore it was not their job to accommodate split families. The message was that it was the sole responsibility of the parents to communicate about their child. While I sort of understand what they were trying to do, it actually caused more problems than it solved: my daughter's mother got fed up of having to contact me all the time when she was trying to build a new life and new family, and I began to feel more and more excluded from my daughter's education, and more and more resentful of my ex and the school. For a while this made communication more strained, which was not fair on my daughter.

Critical questions

»   *Which school do you feel had the more appropriate policy for dealing with separation and divorce?*

»   *What would you include in a whole school policy intended to support teaching staff in dealing with separation and divorce?*

Do not assume that separated parents have worked out how to communicate about their child/children; also, do not assume this makes them unreasonable or, worse, bad parents. This sort of separation and divorce comes about because of a breakdown in a relationship, and even when parents want to put the best interests of their children first they may have differing ideas about how to do this. Encourage both parents to keep you informed about changes to family circumstances that change the living circumstances of the child, eg divorce, new partners, remarriage. This will need to be handled carefully: seek advice from senior staff or family support workers if in doubt as to the best way to do this. Organisations like Gingerbread (www.gingerbread.org.uk/) or Break (www.break-charity.org/) offer advice and support to single parent and separated families, and the National Family Mediation website (www.nfm.org.uk/) has sections for children and teens, parents, step-parents, grandparents, and friends and family.

If a situation has been referred to court you may find yourself having to liaise with social workers or Cafcass (Children and Family Court Support Service), although the latter is only really likely in relation to Section 7 welfare reports. As a result of The Children Act (1989) the courts may ask Cafcass to put together a full welfare report before making a decision regarding access, for example, and at this point you may be contacted depending on the remit of the report. It is important that you are fully aware of your responsibilities in terms of safeguarding, child protection and other statutory frameworks as per Part Two of the Teachers' Standards (DfE, 2011). It is also important that you use the full support network available to you in your school setting to ensure you are following the correct procedures.

Separation due to work or imprisonment

Parents who work away or are serving in the armed forces, or parents sentenced to imprisonment, may spend extended periods away from the family home. This type of separation is different to when parents split up, but it can still be a difficult time for a child, especially if the parent does a high-risk job such as working on oil rigs, a dangerous job like that done by front-line troops in the military, or has been convicted of illegal activity. This can be made worse if they are involved in situations with high levels of media coverage. In these cases it is best to liaise with parents and support agencies, for example, the MOD-funded Children's Education Advisory Service (CEAS) or the Prisoners' Families and Friends Service (PFFS), to establish appropriate ways of supporting pupils in school.

CHECKLIST

Parental separation and changes to family circumstances

✓   Don't judge.

✓   Maintain positive home–school links.

✓   Check the school's policy regarding communication with parents no longer at the same address and adhere to it.

✓   If there is no standard policy then contact both parents and ask how they would prefer to be kept informed of their child/children's progress and school events.

✓   Establish what to do in an emergency, especially if one parent has moved away from the local area.

✓   Make sure your school website and class pages are up to date: for some parents, this may be the only way of hearing about upcoming events.

✓   Unless a court order restricts access to one or both parents, treat both parents equally.

Further reading

HM Government (2011) *Prevent Strategy*. [online] Available at: www.gov.uk/government/uploads/system/uploads/attachment_data/file/97976/prevent-strategy-review.pdf (accessed 8 December 2015).

Littleton, K and Mercer, N (2013) *Interthinking: Putting Talk to Work*. Abingdon: Routledge.

Sources of support

All the websites listed below were valid at the time of going to press.

Cyber safety websites

These are good for keeping your pupils safe online.

www.ceop.police.uk/

www.inspireict.co.uk/e-safety

www.kidsmart.org.uk/

www.saferinternet.org.uk/

www.thegrid.org.uk/eservices/safety/weblinks_parents.shtml

www.thinkuknow.co.uk/

International opportunities

Erasmus+ (if you fancy experiencing teaching abroad or want to internationalise your pupils' curriculum this site is a good first port of call): https://erasmusplus.org.uk/

Professional bodies and subject associations

Association for Language Learning (if you are looking for ideas for language teaching then look no further than this website): www.all-languages.org.uk

Association for Physical Education (AfPE) (provides resources and support in the field of PE including health and safety; the only physical education subject association in the UK): www.afpe.org.uk

Association for Science Education (great support website for science primary teachers): www.ase.org.uk

Association of Teachers of Mathematics (if you are looking for evidence-based research in mathematics then look no further than ATM): www.atm.org.uk

Design and Technology Association (DATA): www.data.org.uk

Geographical Association (subject association for all teachers of geography): www.geography.org.uk

Little Parachutes (website devoted to reviewing picture books that help children deal with a range of difficult issues and situations): www.littleparachutes.com/category.php

Music Mark (high-quality support and ideas for those involved in teaching music): www.musicmark.org.uk

National Association for Primary Education (NAPE) (good for supporting those concerned with children from birth to 13 years): nape.org.uk

National Association for the Teaching of English (NATE) (with ideas for resources, journals, conferences and courses, NATE puts you in touch with the field of English): www.nate.org.uk/

National Centre for Excellence in the Teaching of Mathematics (NCETM) (a vast range of materials to support your subject knowledge and resources to assist you in teaching mathematics): www.ncetm.org.uk

National Association of Teachers of Religious Education (courses and resources for teaching RE): www.natre.org.uk

National Drama: www.nationaldrama.org.uk

NRICH (the NRICH project strives to enrich the mathematical experiences of all learners by providing mathematics resources for pupils, parents and teachers – great for problem-solving ideas): nrich.maths.org/

STEM (a great site for those wanting to enhance their knowledge in science, technology and mathematics): www.nationalstemcentre.org.uk/stem-in-context/professional-development

The Historical Association (aims to further the study, teaching and enjoyment of history at all levels: for both teachers and pupils): www.history.org.uk

UK Literacy Association (UKLA): https://ukla.org/

Social and emotional support

Relate: www.relate.org.uk/relationship-help/help-separation-and-divorce/dealing-childrens-feelings-and-behaviour

The Centre for Separated Families: www.separatedfamilies.info/home/families/

Special needs

Autism Education Trust: www.autismeducationtrust.org.uk/

British Dyslexia Association: www.bdadyslexia.org.uk/information-and-activities/teachers-and-schools.html

Department for Education (DfE) (2014) *Special Educational Needs and Disability Code of Practice: 0 to 25 years. Statutory Guidance for Organisations Who Work With and Support Children and Young People with Special Educational Needs and Disabilities.* Available online at: www.gov.uk/government/publications/send-code-of-practice-0-to-25

Dyspraxia Foundation: www.dyspraxiafoundation.org.uk/dyspraxia-children/

Epilepsy Action: www.epilepsy.org.uk/info/education

The Makaton Charity: www.makaton.org/

Teacher supply and recruitment

Teaching Personnel supplies both teachers and support staff for schools:

www.teachingpersonnel.com/go/schools/

Hays (a big supply teacher agency): www.hays.co.uk/job/education-jobs/supply-teaching/

Unions

NUT: www.teachers.org.uk/ATL: www.atl.org.uk

NASWUT: www.nasuwt.org.uk

Your Initial Teacher Training provider

References

Carter, A (2015) *Carter Review of Initial Teacher Training (ITT)*. [online] Available at: www.gov.uk/government/uploads/system/uploads/attachment_data/file/399957/Carter_Review.pdf (accessed 7 December 2015).

Cotton, K (2001) *Classroom Questioning*. [online] Available at: www.learner.org/workshops/socialstudies/pdf/session6/6.ClassroomQuestioning.pdf (accessed 10 December 2015).

Covey, S (2013) *Seven Habits of Highly Successful People: Powerful Lessons in Personal Change*. London: Simon & Schuster Audio UK.

Dale, R (1997) *Education: Culture, Economy, and Society*. Oxford: Oxford University Press.

Department for Children, Schools and Families (DCSF) (2003) *Every Child Matters* [online] Available at: www.legislation.gov.uk/ukpga/2004/31/contents (accessed 13 October 2015).

Department for Children, Schools and Families (DCSF) (2008) *The Impact of Parental Involvement in Children's Education*. Nottingham: DCSF Publications.

Department for Children, Schools and Families (DCSF) (2009) *Safeguarding Disabled Children: Practice Guidance*. [online] Available at: www.gov.uk/government/uploads/system/uploads/attachment_data/file/190544/00374-2009DOM-EN.pdf (accessed 14 October 2015).

Department for Education (DfE) (2011) *Teachers' Standards: Guidance for School Leaders, School Staff and Governing Bodies*. London: HMSO.

Department for Education (DfE) (2012) *Teacher Appraisal and Capability: A Model Policy for Schools*. [online] Available at www.gov.uk/government/publications/teacher-appraisal-and-capability-model-policy (accessed 12 October 2015).

Department for Education (DfE) (2013a) *Statutory Guidance on Induction for Newly Qualified Teachers (England): For Appropriate Bodies, Head teachers, School Staff and Governing Bodies*. [online] Available at: www.gov.uk/government/uploads/system/uploads/attachment_data/file/269288/induction_for_newly_qualified_teachers.pdf (accessed 29 November 2015).

Department for Education (DfE) (2013b) *Use of Reasonable Force: Advice for Headteachers, Staff and Governing Bodies*. [online] Available at: www.gov.uk/government/publications/use-of-reasonable-force-in-schools (accessed 4 December 2015).

Department for Education (DfE) (2013c) *The National Curriculum in England: Key Stages 1 and 2 Framework Document*. [online] Available at: www.gov.uk/government/uploads/system/uploads/attachment_data/file/425601/PRIMARY_national_curriculum.pdf (accessed 29 November 2015).

Department for Education (DfE) (2014a) *Special Educational Needs and Disability Code of Practice: 0 to 25 years. Statutory Guidance for Organisations Who Work With and Support Children and Young People with Special Educational Needs and Disabilities*. London: HMSO. [online] Available at: www.gov.uk/government/publications/send-code-of-practice-0-to-25 (accessed 15 September 2015).

Department for Education (DfE) (2014b) *Induction for Newly Qualified Teachers (England): Statutory Guidance for Appropriate Bodies, Headteachers, School Staff and Governing Bodies*. London: HMSO. [online] Available at: www.gov.uk/government/publications/induction-for-newly-qualified-teachers-nqts (accessed 15 September 2015).

Department for Education (DfE) (2014c) *Assessment Principles*. [online] Available at: www.gov.uk/government/uploads/system/uploads/attachment_data/file/304602/Assessment_Principles.pdf (accessed 4 December 2015).

Department for Education (DfE) (2014d) *Behaviour and Discipline in Schools: Advice for Headteachers and School Staff*. [online] Available at: www.gov.uk/government/publications/behaviour-and-discipline-in-schools (accessed 4 December 2015).

Department for Education (DfE) (2014e) *School Attendance: Departmental Advice for Maintained Schools, Academies, Independent Schools and Local Authorities*. [online] Available at: www.gov.uk/government/uploads/system/uploads/attachment_data/file/361008/Advice_on_school_attendance_sept_2014.pdf (accessed 24 November 2015).

Department for Education (DfE) (2014f) *The Children and Families Act*. [online] Available at: www.legislation.gov.uk/ukpga/2014/6/pdfs/ukpga_20140006_en.pdf (accessed 14 October 2015).

Department for Education (DfE) (2015a) *Use of Reasonable Force: Advice for Headteachers, Staff and Governing Bodies*. [online] Available at: www.gov.uk/government/uploads/system/uploads/attachment_data/file/444051/Use_of_reasonable_force_advice_Reviewed_July_2015.pdf (accessed 24 November 2015).

Department for Education (DfE) (2015b) *Bullying at School*. [online] Available at: www.gov.uk/bullying-at-school/bullying-a-definition

Department for Education (DfE) (2015c) *The Prevent Duty: Departmental Advice for Schools and Childcare Providers*. Crown copyright DFE-00174-2015.

Department for Education (DfE) (2015d) *School Teachers' Pay and Conditions Document 2015 and Guidance on School Teachers' Pay and Conditions*. Crown copyright DFE-00228-2015.

Department for Education (DfE) and Department of Health (DoH) (2015) *Special Educational Needs Code of Practice: 0–25*. [online] Available at: www.gov.uk/government/uploads/system/uploads/attachment_data/file/398815/SEND_Code_of_Practice_January_2015.pdf (accessed 14 October 2015).

Department for Education and Skills (DfES) (2004) *The Children Act*. [online] Available at: www.legislation.gov.uk/ukpga/2004/31/contents (accessed 12 October 2015).

Department for Education and Skills (DfES) (2006) *Safeguarding Children and Safer Recruitment in Education*. [online] Available at: www.epm.co.uk/downloads/Safeguarding_Children_and_Safer_Recruitment_in_Education_Booklet.pdf (accessed 9 October 2015).

Department of Health (DoH) (2014) *The Care Act*. [online] Available at: www.legislation.gov.uk/ukpga/2014/23/contents/enacted/data.htm (accessed 13 October 2015).

Grigg, R (2010) *Becoming an Outstanding Primary School Teacher*. Harlow: Pearson Education Limited.

HM Government (2015) *Working Together to Safeguard Children: A Guide to Interagency Working to Safeguard and Promote the Welfare of Children*. [online] Available at: www.gov.uk/government/uploads/system/uploads/attachment_data/file/419595/Working_Together_to_Safeguard_Children.pdf (accessed 11 October 2015).

HM Government (no date) *Discrimination: Your Rights*. [online] Available at: www.gov.uk/discrimination-your-rights/types-of-discrimination

Hughes, S, Bingle, B, Crabtree, H, Irving, S, Perrigo, A, Robinson, C, Stanton, J, Watson, R and Whittenbury, J (2011) Mentoring and Coaching Stories: The Learning Journeys of Lecturers Undertaking Post Graduate Study in Mentoring and Coaching. *Worcester Journal of Learning and Teaching*, 6.

Megginson, D and Clutterbuck, D (2005) *Techniques for Coaching and Mentoring*. Oxford: Butterworth-Heinemann.

Mercer, N (2000) *Words and Minds: How We Use Language To Think Together*. London: Routledge.

MESH (no date) *Connecting Educators with Summaries and Sources of Educational Research*. [online] Available at: www.meshguides.org/ (accessed 10 December 2015).

Ofsted (2014) *Initial Teacher Education Inspection Handbook*. Manchester: Ofsted. [online] Available at: www.ofsted.gov.uk/resources/initial-teacher-education-inspection-handbook (accessed 31 August 2014).

Ofsted (2015a) *School Inspection Handbook: Handbook for Inspecting Schools in England under Section 5 of the Education Act 2005*. [online] Available at: www.gov.uk/government/publications/school-inspection-handbook-from-september-2015 (accessed 29 September 2015)

Ofsted (2015b) *Inspecting Schools: A Guide for Parents*. [online] Available at: www.gov.uk/government/uploads/system/uploads/attachment_data/file/457440/School_inspections_-_a_guide_for_parents.pdf (accessed 29 September 2015).

Patty, W and Johnson, L (1953) *Personality and Adjustment*. [online] Available at: www.bartleby.com/73/195.html (accessed 3 December 2015).

Robinson, C (2013) *A Recipe for Effective Mentoring and Coaching of Primary Graduate Teacher Trainees*.

Robinson, C, Bingle, B and Howard, C (2015) *Your Primary School-based Experience: A Guide to Outstanding Placements*. 2nd ed. Northwich: Critical Publishing.

Schon, D (1991) *The Reflective Practitioner: How Professionals Think In Action*. New York, NY: Basic Books.

STEM (no date) *Curriculum: Developing the School Curriculum* [online] Available at: www.nationalstemcentre.org.uk/stem-in-context/curriculum (accessed 27 July 2015).

Whitmore, J (2002) *Coaching for Performance: Growing People, Performance and Purpose.* 3rd ed. London: Nicholas Brealey Publishing Ltd.

Wiliam, D (2004) Assessment and the Regulation of Learning. Paper presented at Invited Symposium *What Does it Mean for Classroom Assessment to be Valid? Reliable?* at the annual meeting of the National Council on Measurement in Education, April 2004, San Diego, CA.

Index